CULTIVATING CURIOSITY

in K–12 Classrooms

ASCD MEMBER BOOK

Many ASCD members received this book as a
member benefit upon its initial release.

Learn more at: **www.ascd.org/memberbooks**

CULTIVATING CURIOSITY

in K-12 Classrooms

How to Promote and Sustain Deep Learning

Wendy L. Ostroff

Alexandria, Virginia USA

1703 N. Beauregard St. • Alexandria, VA 22311-1714 USA
Phone: 800-933-2723 or 703-578-9600 • Fax: 703-575-5400
Website: www.ascd.org • E-mail: member@ascd.org
Author guidelines: www.ascd.org/write

Deborah S. Delisle, *Executive Director*, Robert D. Clouse, *Managing Director, Digital Content & Publications*; Stefani Roth, *Publisher*; Genny Ostertag, *Director, Content Acquisitions*; Julie Houtz, *Director, Book Editing & Production*; Liz Wegner, *Editor*; Masie Chong, *Graphic Designer*; Mike Kalyan, *Manager, Production Services*; BMWW, *Typesetter*; Kelly Marshall, *Senior Production Specialist*

PAPERBACK ISBN: 978-1-4166-2197-3   ASCD product #116001
PDF E-BOOK ISBN: 978-1-4166-2199-7; see Books in Print for other formats.

Quantity discounts: 10–49, 10%; 50+, 15%; 1,000+, special discounts (e-mail programteam@ascd.org or call 800-933-2723, ext. 5773, or 703-575-5773). For desk copies, go to www.ascd.org/deskcopy.

ASCD Member Book No. FY16-8A (July 2016 PSI+). ASCD Member Books mail to Premium (P), Select (S), and Institutional Plus (I+) members on this schedule: Jan, PSI+; Feb, P; Apr, PSI+; May, P; Jul, PSI+; Aug, P; Sep, PSI+; Nov, PSI+; Dec, P. For current details on membership, see www.ascd.org/membership.

Library of Congress Cataloging-in-Publication Data
Ostroff, Wendy L., author.
    Cultivating curiosity in K-12 classrooms : how to promote and sustain deep learning / Wendy L. Ostroff.
    Alexandria, Virginia : ASCD, 2016. | Includes bibliographical references and index.
    LCCN 2016010504 (print) | LCCN 2016011819 (ebook) | ISBN 9781416621973 (pbk. : alk. paper) | ISBN 9781416621997 (PDF)
    LCSH: Teaching. | Curiosity.
    Classification: LCC LB1025.3 .O885 2016 (print) | LCC LB1025.3 (ebook) | DDC 371.102--dc23
LC record available at http://lccn.loc.gov/2016010504

25 24 23 22 21 20 19 18 17 16   1 2 3 4 5 6 7 8 9 10 11 12

CULTIVATING CURIOSITY

in K-12 Classrooms

Acknowledgments

So many people have contributed to this project. It is no exaggeration to say that there would be no book without them! I would first like to thank Richard Papale and Genny Ostertag from ASCD for the conversations that nourished the idea and the freedom to delve in and flesh it out. I would also like to thank my wonderful editor at ASCD, Liz Wegner.

I am indebted to those who shared their thoughts and references, stories and talents, including Hannah Lee Marik, Tony Mountain, Cécile LePage, Patty Kean, Eric Common, Sebastien Bernard, Tony Kashani, Rachel Treat, Leah Amaru, Buzz Kellogg, Melanie Dana, Michael Leras, and Susan Ruckle.

I would like to thank the faculty of the Hutchins School of Liberal Studies for ever-prioritizing imagination and risk taking in their classrooms, and for welcoming me back. And I especially want to thank my students for their presence and intellectual playfulness day in and day out, around the seminar tables of Carson Hall.

I would like to offer a huge thank you to Heidi Ostroff, Jane Ostroff-Lin, and Carmen and Carol Genova for giving me the gift of time. And of course, thanks to my parents, David and Susanne Ostroff, for cultivating the original seeds of curiosity in my brain by way of books and projects.

I am enormously grateful to Margaret Anderson for her magical powers in dialogue, telempathy, and articulation, which helped me think through and weave together this narrative (not to mention every other narrative over which I have puzzled). And thank you to the philosopher-questioners, including Eleanor Ostroff, Mutombo M'Panya, Ben Frymer, Fay Afaf Kanafani, Karen Hurka-Richardson, Francisco Vázquez, and Bob Brocken, who are closest to me in mind and heart.

Without a doubt, the deepest gratitude belongs to Rob Genova, who matched the time spent on this book nearly hour for hour. Thank you always and ever, Rob, for your experimental nature and for filling my life with love, life, and authentic possibility.

Finally, I would like to thank the most awake and curious people I know, Alexei Carmen Genova and Sonia Cécile Genova. May you always allow yourselves to be swept away with those things you notice and wonder about. This book (and all the love that went into it) is for you.

Introduction

How to Cultivate the Curiosity Classroom

What we want to see is the child in pursuit of knowledge, not knowledge in pursuit of the child.

—George Bernard Shaw,
The Quintessence of G.B.S.

Learning is what we humans do best. We learn throughout our lives by wondering and exploring, experiencing and playing. This book is about harnessing that ineffable drive in learners—the drive to know, understand, and engage in the world and its ideas. The philosopher Cicero defined curiosity as a love of knowledge without the lure of profit (1914), in other words, an intrinsic passion to know. Aristotle (1947) claimed that the desire to know is among the deepest human urges, and Francis Crick, the Nobel Prize–winning scientist who discovered the structure of DNA, was often described as childlike in his curiosity (Pincock, 2004).

Curiosity has been hailed as the major impetus behind cognitive development, education, and scientific discovery (Loewenstein, 1994).

It is the drive that brings learners to knowledge. Curiosity is about being aware and open, checking things out, experimenting, and interacting within one's surroundings. In a classroom grounded in curiosity, teachers have the unique opportunity of being able to mine students' deepest held wonder, making their attention natural and effortless, and allowing them to fully engage. Creating the conditions for curiosity in the classroom will allow us to achieve more authentic motivation from both teachers and students, leading to deeper learning.

It is no wonder that Curious George is one of the most beloved characters in children's literature. The little monkey who lives with the Man with the Yellow Hat wants to dig into each and every experience he comes across in order to explore and to experiment. And he often gets into trouble, especially because he is not limited by the things that are socially appropriate. He is free to do what he chooses, and is a monkey, after all, filled with all the monkey-shines we might expect. It is a good thing that Curious George has the Man with the Yellow Hat to save him from the tricky situations he gets himself into (to come by in a helicopter at just the right moment when George floats too high on a bunch of balloons, for instance). In the case of George, just as in the case of our students, playful curiosity plus scaffolding can transform into learning.

We don't need to teach our students to be curious—like George, they are already curious. (Though they may not be curious about what we want them to be curious about.) Maybe at this moment they are wondering how the clay feels in a kindergarten classroom readying for a project or wondering how to talk to a friend they have a crush on in a middle school science lab. Are there learning moments that a skilled guide can find at the intersection between what the students are curious about and the topics at hand? Can we take our students' interest in skateboarding on a half-pipe and direct it into an interest in physics or engineering? Can we use their interest in persuading their parents to get a pet and mold it into skills in persuasive writing or speaking? In this book, I will make the case that students' curiosity coupled with teachers' own wonder and experience can guide students into deeper inquiry.

Why Curiosity?

Being curious is an essential part of human consciousness, a joyful feature of a life well lived. But as recent research evidence shows, fostering curiosity holds a power that goes beyond merely feeling good. In fact, curiosity may be critical to student success in school. What are the mechanisms by which curiosity compels learning?

1. Curiosity Jump-Starts and Sustains Intrinsic Motivation, Allowing Deep Learning to Happen with Ease

When students are curious, teaching and learning are never a chore. Whereas motivation that comes from the outside (via incentives and rewards) tends to be fragile and short-lived, motivation that comes from inside ourselves, from the wellspring of genuine curiosity, is much like a wild fire: It cannot be tamed, it will take sudden new turns or directions, and it will seek fuel in whatever way it can. In a classroom based on students' curiosity, teachers needn't ever worry about motivation.

When children are allowed to follow their curiosity, they are more likely to stay on the path of exploration and insight. For example, a 1st grader's discovery of tadpoles in a marshy puddle in the play yard brings her immediate joy. That joy ignites the spark of curiosity, and she is then intrinsically motivated to further explore the puddle, since pleasure compels repetition. The girl may bring her classmates to see the puddle, or she may decide to look for tadpoles in other small ponds after school. In either case, she will seek to branch her experience outward. On each occasion that she returns to observe the tadpoles, she will pose questions and make hypotheses about them ("What do they eat?" or "How fast or far can they swim?"), with repeated observations guiding her mastery. The child will soon observe the tadpoles growing stubs of legs, and if she is allowed to continue to watch, she will witness the complex biological transformation of tadpoles becoming frogs. Her mastery of the topic, gained from experiential learning, will produce confidence. As this example illustrates, the movement into deep learning is fueled by curiosity and pleasure (Perry, 2001).

Research shows that any student, given the opportunity to be genuinely curious, will respond in precisely the same way. In one study, groups of 5th and 6th graders learned about endangered wolves or coal mining in class. The first group participated in a group discussion on the facts they had learned, while the second group entered into a debate about the controversies surrounding wolves becoming endangered or the strip mining of coal. In this case, as in other studies, the "seductive details" of the controversy sparked curiosity. The second group not only showed more enthusiasm during the project, they spent significantly more time working on it and were more likely to give up a recess period to learn more about the topic (Lowry & Johnson, 1981). The increased time spent engaging with these topics inevitably led students to delve more deeply into them, which helped students understand the complex concepts better and remember the content later (see also Garner, Brown, Sanders, & Menke, 1992).

2. Curiosity Releases Dopamine, Which Not Only Brings Pleasure but Also Improves Observation and Memory

The brain's desire and reward system (the producer of the neurotransmitter dopamine) is deeply embedded in our human development and evolution. Since social scientists believe that reward drives all behavior, and behavior creates evolutionary adaptation, the dopamine system has been critical in our evolution into the complex beings we are (Muller, 2014).

When students are curious and seek to satisfy their goals and desires, they get a hit of this pleasure-producing chemical. In one study on the effects of dopamine, people were given a list of trivia questions, like "Who was the president of the United States when Uncle Sam first got a beard?" or "What does the term 'dinosaur' actually mean?" and then asked how curious they were to learn each answer. They then were given brain scans while being presented with both the answers to the trivia questions and additional unrelated information. When the participants' curiosity was triggered, their brains released dopamine. Upon being tested afterwards, participants were much more likely to remember information on the topics they were curious about. In addition, when participants were in a curious state, they were also more likely to remember the paired, unrelated information. In other words, when we are curious, our brains' surge in dopamine causes us to take in and remember the entire landscape of experience and information more deeply. This is because dopamine makes the hippocampus (the part of the brain associated with long-term memory) function better (Gruber, Gelman, & Ranganath, 2014). Such research lends support to what nature writer John Burroughs observed nearly a century ago: "Knowledge without love does not stick; but if love comes first, knowledge is pretty sure to follow" (1919, p. 28).

3. Curious People Exhibit Enhanced Cognitive Skills

Curious students learn more and learn better. Current research shows that people who nurture the tendency to seek new information and experiences show lasting brain effects. In one study, researchers identified a group of 3-year-olds who were extra curious and followed their development throughout their childhood and school experiences. At 11 years of age, these children were earning significantly higher grades than their peers. They were superior readers and had IQ scores that averaged 12 points higher than their less curious counterparts (Raine, Reynolds, Venables, & Mednick, 2002).

In a related study at the other end of the lifespan, scientists discovered that older adults who were genetically predisposed to develop Alzheimer's disease, but who kept curiosity a daily part of their lives, warded off the disease for more than a decade. In particular, seeking out higher education, working in complex fields, playing music, avidly reading, and staying intellectually engaged created a recipe for keeping the brain effective and healthy (Vemuri et al., 2014).

The Curiosity Classroom Is Co-Created

When we as teachers recognize that we are partners with our students in life's long and complex journey, when we begin to treat them with the dignity and respect they deserve for simply being, then we are on the road to becoming worthy teachers. It is just that simple—and just that difficult.

—William Ayers, "The Mystery of Teaching," in *The Jossey-Bass Reader on Teaching*

Teachers play a critical role in helping students transform their curiosity into inquiry, by facilitating, focusing, challenging, and encouraging students in active engagement (Zion & Slezak, 2005). When a teacher guides students into new, related territory, expanding upon the interests of those students and branching them out, we call it scaffolding (Rogoff, 1990). Scaffolding supports those goals that the student can stretch to achieve with a bit of help but that he or she would be unable to reach alone (Vygotsky, 1934/1998). Again, supporting curious children is best achieved when teachers themselves are curious, when they are excited, involved, self-directed, and trying new things (Deci & Ryan, 1985; Engel, 2011; Ostroff, 2012). In that way, the curiosity classroom creates a culture of learning that emerges at the intersection of the students and the teacher.

Curiosity is cultivated within classroom walls as a shared endeavor involving both students and teachers as learners. It is a collaborative search beginning with ideas and questions from the lived situations of all members (Greene, 1995). Fostering curiosity involves listening to the myriad of voices and perspectives of the class community members and respecting each other enough to put oneself "out there." Writer and teacher Parker Palmer (2003) has said that teaching is a daily exercise in vulnerability. Peers, too, take a risk by being present and prepared for the classroom setting based on curiosity. As one Brookline, Massachusetts, high school student put it, you don't just get what you put into it, you get what the entire class puts into it (Kohn, 1993).

Curiosity is by nature subversive to the traditional, top-down classroom. When order in the classroom is desired most of all, curiosity can become a liability. After all, hunger and seeking are not obedient and tame. In a now-famous review of decades of psychological research, George Loewenstein (1994) discovered that curiosity was most associated with intensity, transience, and impulsivity, all three of which tend to be discouraged in hierarchical classrooms. Formal instruction has typically been designed to control dynamic and propulsive students, like that precocious child who ignores the lesson while focusing on a mission of her own (Shonstrom, 2014). Curious kids criticize systems; they play; they jab at authority. Curiosity may not be radiating from the good boy or girl in the front of the class, but it may be from the kid in back, near the window, giving us heartburn with his attitude (Seal, 1995). Social critic Jennifer Fink (2015) writes,

While my son still needs movement, still craves real-world learning, physical labor and ways to contribute to his family and his world, he's expected to spend most of his time in a desk, in a classroom, with 20-some other kids his age. He's not allowed to go outside at school when it's too cold or wet; he's expected to sit quietly in the library or auditorium during recess time. He's allowed few opportunities for "real" work; today, when you hand an 8-year-old a saw or allow him to start a fire, people look at you askance. One hundred and fifty years ago, my son would have been considered a model boy. Today, more often than not, he's considered a troublemaker.

For students to be able to express curiosity, they must feel entitled to ask and to seek, even if that means going against the grain and straying a bit in their explorations. In fact, curiosity is highly malleable. As educators, each of us has the power to nurture or crush it in others. For our most at-risk students, time to wonder and wander is essential. Not surprisingly, these students (of whom society expects the least) have had their curiosity the most dulled by rote learning, high restrictions, and classrooms focused on obedience. The only hope for these at-risk kids—and all kids—is to reinstate curiosity in our schools, by disengaging the education system from standardization—both in curricula and assessment (Shonstrom, 2014).

In order not to squash what comes naturally to students, we must allow for what philosopher Hannah Arendt called "the startling unexpectedness of all beginnings" (1961, p. 169), and what educational philosopher John Dewey (1916) called venturing into the unknown. The journey is equally as important for teachers as it is for students. Once we view ourselves as learners and explorers, more and more new things begin to seem possible (Greene, 1995). This represents a shift in the way we see the traditional role of a teacher, from one who asks and answers the questions, to one who elicits them. When science teacher Mark Knapp decided to do a unit on astronomy with his 6th graders, he knew almost nothing about astronomy, and told his class so. One kid exclaimed, "So now you're going to teach us something you know nothing about?" and Mark retorted, "You bet I am! Any homework that I assign you, I am going to do, myself. We're going to have a blast learning this together" (Fried, 2003, p. 111). Indeed, the curiosity classroom provides space for authentic and emergent experiences, possibility, and sense of ownership. This book is about empowering teachers to bring out and sustain curiosity in their students and to create a classroom in which it thrives.

When the teacher is a co-learner, the knowledge and insight that the students bring to the classroom is just as important, and equally worthy to learn, as that of the teachers (Freire, 1998). This doesn't mean that teachers need to let children's every question and moment of tinkering derail the lesson plan. But they can plan significant portions of the curriculum around the goal of inviting and encouraging children to pursue their curiosity, helping children figure out just what it is they want to know, and then showing them how to systematically go about getting the answers to their investigations and explorations. One of the most valuable functions a teacher can serve is to help children become more aware of, and deliberate about, their curiosity. Teacher Melissa Parent uses the KWL approach—What do we *know*? What do we *want* to know? And what have we *learned*?—to build her curriculum. For example, for an upcoming science unit on sound, she let her students know, "We need to study sound, but you get to decide what we learn about." This allowed her to focus her lesson prep on the aspects of sound that the class was genuinely interested in. She told them, "You are the designer of this unit" and reminded them that she's new to teaching and has a lot to learn herself. They knew immediately that she would not just be teaching things to them—that they would be learning things together (Fried, 2003, p. 119).

As teacher Carolyn Edwards points out, teaching as a co-learner is not about making things smooth or easy for the students. Quite the contrary. Teacher facilitators stimulate learning by making problems more complex, involved, and stimulating (Edwards, 1993). Helping students to follow their own interests and guide them in inquiry takes patience and hard work. "I'm in control of putting students in control," is how one educator put it—a responsibility that is much more complex than simply telling students what to do (Kohn, 1993).

The "We" Rather Than the "I"

Co-creating a curiosity classroom requires some degree of humility. Teachers have to cease being in charge and listen to the multitude of voices in the classroom with equal respect. One of the greatest novelists of all time, Leo Tolstoy, did something akin to this when he opened free schools—without programs, punishments, or rules—for local peasant children. In his piece "Who Should Learn Writing of Whom: Peasant Children of Us, or We from Peasant Children?" Tolstoy (1862/2015) described the barely literate children he worked with from the streets, whose self-awareness in writing and complexity in ideas rivaled his own. Learning from them was first strange and humiliating, but ultimately liberating, as Tolstoy and the children began to cowrite their stories. "Someone said, let's make this old man a wizard; someone else said, no, we don't need to do that, let him be just a soldier; no better have him rob them; no, that wouldn't fit the proverb" (p. 302). As soon as Tolstoy put his ego aside and stopped trying to instruct them, all children participated in writing the story. They became carried away with the process of creation itself, and this was the first step in the direction of inspiration. The children composed plotlines, created the characters, described their appearances in great detail, and invented individual episodes, all in clear linguistic form. The work was a true collaborative effort, in which the children felt themselves to be equal partners with an adult. Children spent sun up to sun down at their studies, and at the end of the day, they were still reluctant to leave the schoolhouse (Ashton-Warner, 2003). Tolstoy concluded that authentic education involves awakening in the child what already exists within him, and simply helping him to develop it (Vygotsky, 1967/2004).

When planning lessons, we must consider both our own objectives and goals and those of the students. Says one high school teacher, "Spending time on student generated interests is always much more gratifying and effective teaching in my opinion. Years later, it is often those moments that students have told me are the most memorable for them." When implementing lesson plans, we need to consider the learning goals that the students will have for themselves, as well as those we will have for them. Both sets of goals can be built upon the students' previous learning experiences. During assessment, documentation, and evaluation

Quick Recap

▶ All students–indeed, all humans–are curious.

▶ Supporting and scaffolding curiosity opens learners up to knowledge.

▶ Students' and teachers' curiosity can be combined to co-create a curiosity classroom.

▶ Creating a curiosity classroom shifts the traditional views of teaching and learning.

we can gather evidence of the effectiveness of the curriculum by identifying what was learned from both the teacher and student perspective (Wood & Attfield, 2005).

A Few Small Shifts

If the goal of school is innovation, creativity, and authentic progress, curiosity is a blessing. Curious children (i.e., all children) take risks, are intellectually playful, try things out, make productive mistakes, and learn deeply (Leslie, 2014). It takes just a few minor adjustments to transform any classroom into a hotbed of curiosity, beginning with a shift in how teachers view themselves, from teachers to teacher-learners who are curious in their own right about the processes of facilitating learning. In a way, doing this means setting up the classroom to support those skills that all learners begin with, such as the drive to explore, effortless learning, imagination, and intrinsic motivation. Finally, teachers must arrange the time, space, and orientation of the lessons in such a way for these inherent skills to bloom.

Children are superb learners. Each and every student is part of an evolutionary and developmental trajectory of learning that is structured into their biology and cultural context. When provided with the freedom and scaffolding to pursue their own interests, they can and will become efficient, joyful super-learners (Gray, 2013). In what ways are children inherently curious, and how can we support and extend that curiosity?

Small movements in perspective can transform the classroom into a container for an exciting new mode of learning together to happen. When students retain inherent curiosity and wonder, they will first go about asking questions, then seek ways of knowing and approach answers, and finally, begin again with more questions. When students adopt these habits of mind, they are unable to be stopped from learning throughout their lives. Teachers suddenly find themselves being surprised again, asking questions again, remembering what it was that they were so curious about once upon a time, and having a lot of fun. In the meantime, they begin creating a space where the most essential skills for deep learning are germinated—the curiosity classroom.

1

Promote Exploration and Experimentation

We shall not cease from exploration, and the end of all our exploring will be to arrive where we started and know the place for the first time.

—T. S. Eliot

The seeds of curiosity lie in exploring. Right from birth, children are agents of their own learning. Exploration is the act of seeking novelty. It involves experiencing the world in order to gain knowledge. How do young organisms come to be so immediately and fundamentally curious?

The Evolution of Curiosity: Exploratory Reflex

In the 1860s, German zoologist Alfred Brehm placed a covered box of snakes in the cage of several monkeys living in a zoo. When the monkeys lifted the lid, they were terrified, which is the typical reaction of monkeys to snakes. But then they did something rather odd (so odd that Charles Darwin was compelled to recreate the experiment himself). In spite of their fear, the monkeys could not resist reopening the lid of box to take another look at the snakes (Darwin, 1874). Since the publication of these findings in the book *Brehm's Life of Animals* (1864/2015), scientists have tested more than one hundred species of reptiles and mammals on their reactions to never-before-seen things. In all cases, the animals cannot resist novelty. In fact, attention to novelty is a fundamental feature of behavior shared by almost all organisms possessing nervous systems (Pisula, 2009). Novelty compels us to engage with different things, helping us survive by making sure that we pay attention to anything in our environment that can help or harm us.

Experimental psychologists in the last half-century have been fascinated with motivation as a prerequisite for learning. They have discovered that when we come in contact with ambiguous, complex, or conflicting information, our nervous systems become aroused, amping us up and forcing us to pay attention. When we are puzzled, we find a resolution very rewarding, which sets us up for efficient learning (Berlyne, 1966; Loewenstein, 1994). Neuroscientists have begun using functional magnetic resonance imaging (fMRI) to measure brain activation during new and interesting situations. When someone is curious, the brain areas underlying autonomic arousal and discomfort are more highly activated (e.g., the anterior insula and anterior cingulate cortex). Then, when the question at hand is satisfied, that is, when we gain access to relevant information, the brain regions associated with reward are activated (Jepma, Verdonschot, van Steenbergen, Rombouts, & Nieuwenhuis, 2012).

In the realm of human genetics, curiosity and a preference for newness have been linked to the migration of early humans to the far reaches of the earth. As we know, the first humans evolved in Africa about 150,000 years ago. About 100,000 years later, there was a major human migration out of Africa, with humans inhabiting all parts of the globe by about 12,000 years ago. Interestingly, recent studies have shown that those human groups who migrated the furthest from Africa also had a greater frequency of the genes linked to novelty seeking (specifically, the DRD4 exon 3 gene alleles 2R and 7R)

(Lehman & Stanley, 2011; Pisula, Turlejski, & Charles, 2013). In other words, the people who traveled the furthest from their origins may have had some biological propensity to check out and explore mysterious new places and things. As their brains grew larger, humans adapted by seeking out newness and engaging with exciting, novel experiences as a way to learn about the unknown.

The Development of Curiosity: Novel Places and Things

All wonder is the effect of novelty on ignorance.
—Samuel Johnson, *The Works of Samuel Johnson, LL.D.*

Just as curiosity underpins the movement and growth of groups of humans throughout evolutionary time, curiosity is also the driving force behind the growth and movement of each individual child in developmental time. Newborn babies come into the world able to hear, see, feel, taste, and touch things in their surroundings. Their sensory and nervous systems have evolved to respond to the demands of the world with spontaneous and involuntary actions (e.g., the sucking reflex, which ensures that infants will drink milk and be nourished). Reflexes are fixed action patterns that only last a short time, but they slowly turn into other more complex setups for learning. The greater the knowledge of the environment an infant has gained through curiosity, the more the possibility of adaptation to that environment (Kirkpatrick, 1903/2009). In fact, scientists at the National Institute of Child Health and Human Development recently discovered that the more energetically 5-month-old infants explored their surroundings, the more likely they were to perform well in school throughout childhood, all the way to high school (Bornstein, Hahn, & Suwalsky, 2013).

Babies marvel at sights, sounds, and patterns; they manipulate objects to test their physical properties; they stroke and mouth textures. Infants' tendency to be curious comes from the way their nervous systems are set up, and just as with animals, the exploratory drive springs from a perceptual preference for novelty. When given the choice, babies consistently look at, listen to, or play with things they have never experienced before (Diamond, 1995; Lipton & Spelke, 2003). One of the best moments in my early parenthood was catching my baby son noticing his hands for the first time. This discovery stands out like a metaphor for all of the learning experiences to come—his immediate and lasting interest in what those strange and wonderful appendages could do was his first step toward managing to control them. Novelty preference is an efficient way for infants' and young children's immature cognitive systems to process information. Novelty preference helps infants handle environmental changes. It then develops into the insatiable urge to explore and experience new things.

Children, like infants, spend their days in wonder. They can be counted on to open boxes and drawers, peek underneath furniture, and manipulate everything they can. Children make it their business to notice and observe, unearth and manipulate all of the things that might afford action. They use as many sensory systems as possible as a means to know, understand, and master their worlds, sometimes even without realizing it. As my toddler daughter Sonia so eloquently said after being told not to play with a porcelain vase at her great-grandmother's house, "I wasn't touching it, I was just looking at it with my hands."

Children's curiosity swells as they continue to explore, and this curious orientation can underpin engagement throughout K–12 education and beyond. For instance, one study showed that when elementary school-age children read books on topics *they were already wondering about*, they learned significantly more—including picking out more details and retaining what they read for longer periods of time (Engel, 2011). In another study, high school students showed increased engagement and increased enjoyment across school subjects when (1) they were appropriately challenged, (2) they were in control of how they spent their time, and (3) the in-subject activities were relevant to their own interests (Shernoff, Csikszentmihalyi, Schneider, & Shernoff, 2003). Furthermore, adolescents with widespread curiosity and interest in everyday life (including school) experience significantly better health and well-being (Hunter & Csikszentmihalyi, 2003).

Children's Brains Are Optimized for Exploration and Experimentation

Seong Min moved to the United States from Korea at age 4, when her father became a graduate student in chemistry. At first, she would sit timidly in the corner of her preschool classroom, venturing over to a table once in a while to draw or have a snack between tears. With virtually no knowledge of English it was difficult for her teachers to know what Seong Min was thinking or how well she was adjusting. Within about one month, Seong Min was no longer crying and gravitating to the corner of the room. She was playing with the kids outside and participating in the learning centers. By the end of four months, Seong Min was speaking English fluently and participating fully in the classroom! How was she able to learn so quickly?

Both children's and adults' brains are constantly wired and rewired (altered in their structure and function) as they encounter new experiences, understanding, and knowledge (Hensch, 2004). This is called neuroplasticity. Since early experiences have enhanced and longer lasting impacts on the brain (or "optimal neuroplasticity"), youth is the ripest learning period of the lifespan (Knudsen, 2004; Thompson-Schill, Ramscar, & Chrysikou, 2009; White, Hutka, Williams, & Moreno, 2013). It is no wonder children are curious to the core—novelty, exploration, and experimentation are wired in them!

During infancy and childhood, neurons (the cells of the brain) are ultra-sensitive to patterns in sensory input in their environments. Perceptual systems (like seeing, smelling, hearing, and touching) zoom in on, pick up, and organize the features of the child's world. Those pieces of information that are experienced regularly (e.g., the sounds of one's native language) are prioritized in the brain. This means that their neural representations become refined, tuning the child's perceptual systems in to only those specific types of stimulation and input (Kuhl & Rivera-Gaxiola, 2008; Werker & Tees, 1984).

At birth, infants can tell the difference between any sound in any of the world's languages. They can clearly hear the difference between /r/ and /l/, for example, when someone says /rock/ or /lock/. This skill functions to optimize learning language in the first year of life (Werker & Tees, 2005). By 1 year old, however, infants' ability to discriminate sounds in any of the world's languages declines, attuning them to only those sounds that they have been exposed to in their native language (Werker & Tees, 1984). The young brain has now been modified to hear only the necessary sounds and preferentially responds to them. Likewise, adults cannot discriminate or even hear differences in sounds that are not used in their native languages. This is why adult native speakers of many Asian languages have difficulty with the /r/ versus /l/ distinction in English. As a native speaker of English, no matter how carefully I listen or concentrate, I cannot hear the difference between the Hindi dental "d" sound in [dal] (which is a type of lentil), and the retroflex "d" sound in [ḍal] (which is a tree branch). My brain is fully attuned to the sounds I have grown up hearing in English (Kuhl, 2004; Werker & Tees, 1984).

Whereas it was incredibly quick and easy for 4-year-old Seong Min to learn to speak English, it took close to five years for her mother, Ji-Hye, to become fluent, and she was never able to speak like a native. Children who are introduced to a foreign language before the age of 7 can seamlessly pick up the grammar and phonology of the language and speak it without an accent. After age 7, the ease of learning new languages gradually declines until adulthood, regardless of the amount of experience with the new language, motivation to learn, cultural identification, or self-consciousness (Johnson & Newport, 1989). Like languages, early experience in music optimizes the child's brain to perceive and respond to new information. In fact, research has shown that most of history's prodigious musicians, such as Wolfgang Amadeus Mozart, Jimi Hendrix, and Yo-Yo Ma, began training before the age of 7 (White et al., 2013). These findings highlight what many parents and teachers have observed anecdotally: the younger the child, the more effortless the learning. This is because young brains are set up to explore and take in novel information.

Quick Recap

▶ Humans and animals reflexively seek out novelty.

▶ Being curious is evolutionarily adaptive.

▶ Infants and children have an insatiable urge to explore, know, understand, and master their worlds.

▶ Young brains are optimized for new information and change, making infants and children superior learners to older learners.

▶ Children's brains are optimized to learn from exploration and experimentation, not from passively listening to teachers.

Neuroscientist Jay Giedd studies how the human brain develops from birth through adolescence; he has clearly shown that for children younger than 7 or 8, learning via active exploration is far superior to learning from teacher-led explanation: "The trouble with over-structuring is that it discourages exploration," he says (Kohn, 2015, p. 4). Young brains thrive on the exploration and experimentation that are manifested in curiosity.

Scaffolding Exploration and Experimentation in the Classroom

The way that teachers feel about curiosity directly influences the way that their students explore and inquire. In one telling study, 3- and 4-year-olds were invited to play with a toy farm set while an experimenter sat nearby and behaved either in a friendly, encouraging way or an aloof, critical way. The children were then asked to guess what toys they were feeling, hidden behind a curtain. Children who had interacted with a friendly, approving experimenter were much quicker to begin exploring. They spent more time manipulating the toys they could not see, and they were more likely to guess the identity of the hidden object at the end of the session. In contrast, children who had had an aloof, critical experimenter showed significantly less task-related curiosity and exploratory behavior (Moore & Bulbulian, 1976).

In another study, researchers created a box with small novel objects in each of the drawers. They then put the box in kindergarten and 3rd grade classrooms and watched to see who came up to it, how many drawers each child opened, and how long each child spent examining the objects inside the drawers. What these researchers discovered was that in certain classrooms, 3rd graders were equally as curious as kindergartners: Just as many came up to the box quickly, opened all the drawers, and manipulated the contents. Children in both grades played with the little objects equally as long. But in other classrooms, regardless of grade, few children investigated the box. These classrooms, welcoming as they seemed at first glance, were places much less conducive to exploration. The researchers later discovered that there was a direct link between how much the teacher smiled and encouraged students and the level of curiosity the children expressed (Hackmann & Engel, 2002, cited in Engel, 2011).

Some teachers feel that they do not have the freedom or the time to allow children to get off-task and that following the children's interests or indulging tangents is a luxury that they cannot afford because they must ensure that students perform well on standardized tests. In a recent observation of kindergarten, 1st grade, and 5th grade classrooms, when the teachers relegated stretches of time to achieving very specific learning objectives, there just was not time for curiosity (Engel, 2011). How can teachers work within prescribed content standards *and* still encourage exploration and experimentation? The answer may simply be a matter of shifting our implicit attitudes toward curiosity.

In an interesting study with 8- and 9-year-olds, researchers emulated a school science project called The Bouncing Raisins (adding raisins to a mix of vinegar and baking soda, with the delightful result of the raisins bouncing up to the top of the glass) (Engel & Labella, 2011). At the end of the activity, the experimenter responded to the children differently. For half the children, she said something like, "You know what? I wonder what would happen if we dropped one of these [picking up a Skittle from the table] in the liquid instead of a raisin?" With the other half of the children, instead of picking up a Skittle and dropping it in, she simply cleaned the work area up a little, commenting as she did it, "I'm just going to tidy up a bit. I'll put these materials over here." Then the experimenter left the room. As she left, she said, "Feel free to do whatever you want while you are waiting for me. You can use the materials more, or draw with these crayons, or just wait. Whatever you want to do is fine." Children who had seen their guide deviate from the task to satisfy her own curiosity were much more likely to play with the materials, dropping raisins, Skittles, and other items into the liquid, stirring it, and adding other ingredients. Children who instead had seen her tidy up tended to do nothing at all while they waited. The lesson of this research is clear: Teachers' own behavior has a powerful effect on a child's disposition to explore (Engel & Labella, 2011).

Then, these researchers recreated the study, but this time designed it to measure how *teachers* would respond to spontaneous curiosity and exploration on the part of a child. In this case, teachers who volunteered to be participants were all asked to do the experiment with a "student" who was really working with the experimenters. The first group of teachers was told that the focus of the lesson was learning about science. The second group of teachers was told that the focus of the lesson was filling out a worksheet. The task with the jumping raisins was exactly the same, but this time the child (who was a part of the study) was instructed to stray from the instructions and put a Skittle into the glass. If the teacher asked the child what she was doing, the student was trained to reply, "I just wanted to see what would happen" (p. 191). The results were striking. Teachers who believed that the goal of the lesson was learning about science responded with interest and encouragement to the child's diversion, saying things like, "Oh, what are you trying?" or "Maybe we should see what this will do." But those teachers who had been subtly encouraged to focus on completing the worksheet said things like, "Oh wait a second, that's not on the instruction sheet" or "Whoops, that doesn't go in there." Like all humans, teachers are very susceptible to external influences. In this study, teachers' understanding of the goal of a block of time directly impacted how they responded when children wanted to spontaneously investigate (Engel & Randall, 2009).

Quick Recap

▶ Children with warm and encouraging teachers are more likely to explore their environments.

▶ A classroom's culture determines whether or not children will explore, regardless of age or grade level.

▶ When teachers model wonder and encourage spontaneous exploration, students are more willing to experiment.

Curiosity Technique to Try: Discovery Learning

Students benefit from the extra time it takes to discover on their own, even through trial and error. Often in my seminar courses, my students will spend a lot of time hashing out ideas. It is tempting to stop them, especially if they are not on the "right track." For example, in my Biased Brain course, I find it difficult to hear incorrect attempts about brain functionality such as, "Maybe this is how the brain works . . ." when I have more experience with the research literature. But I have to be patient and let them explore so they can discover insights and meaning on their own.

In the same spirit, 8th grade science teacher Muriel Hasek designs labs that are purposefully left open, so that her students can genuinely experiment with the materials and come to their own conclusions. For example, when she wanted her class to understand the properties of solutes and solvents, she just asked the students to begin mixing the liquids however they chose. The students devised their own systematic ways of testing the properties of the liquids and arrived at the understanding she had hoped for (that mixed solutions take on the characteristics of solvents), albeit in very divergent ways. Mistakes were a part of that process, but the goal went far beyond knowing properties of liquids to fostering an experimental mind frame. The next time you design a lesson with an intended discovery for the students, give them the opportunity to get in and muck around a bit. Let them know that finding answers is not always the goal, but the process of discovery can be just as rewarding.

Curiosity Technique to Try: *Choose Your Own Adventure* Lessons

Edward Packard always enjoyed telling his children bedtime stories. But when the fantastical plotlines became more complex, and he ran out of ideas, Edward began giving his kids choices: "Should the character walk through that door, or run the other way?" It didn't take long for him to realize that the children loved his stories all the more when *they* had a say in how the plots turned out. The interactive format became a storytelling device; it both locked in their attention and took advantage of their inherent creativity (Rossen, 2014). The *Choose Your Own Adventure* book series was officially launched in 1979. Children were suddenly allowed to become the main characters themselves—they were put in control while embodying the deep-sea explorer or the surgeon or the mountain climber ("If you put up the energy repulsion shields to try and escape the black hole, turn to page 22!"). They made choices—and that made them want to read.

You can design a lesson plan on the same premise. In biology, for example, a lesson on cells could lead students to six or seven different paths depending on their interests. Ask students to identify the parts of a plant cell under the microscope. Then, after labeling their diagram, they come to a choice point: "If you want to look at animal cells now, go to Table #2 and put an animal slide on" or "If you want to understand more deeply how the mitochondria work, go the computer research station and seek out some more information and images. Draw what you find." After seeing both animal and plant cells, they may have a choice to learn more about the history of the microscope, or to compare the cells of various animals or plants. They may have an option to create a more stylized image that integrates the parts of both a plant and animal cell at an art table. They can choose their level of analysis, zooming in or out, or moving laterally into new ways to discover cells based on their own interests. Your students will be engaged and excited to see where they wind up.

In Sum

Curiosity is at the heart of how humans change, learn, and grow—both in developmental and evolutionary time scales. Being biologically drawn to novelty helps us deal with changes in our environments and guides our attention to things we can discover, explore, and understand. When learners satisfy the urge to know, they feel really satisfied because they are activating the brain regions responsible for reward and pleasure. Young children's brains are most malleable and therefore are the most profoundly influenced by new experiences. Children are more superior learners than adults when it comes to some of the most complex and abstract concepts, like language and music.

When students' curiosity is activated, they learn more, and they learn better. Research shows that children's learning skyrockets when they read about things they are already wondering about, or when their active and spontaneous exploration guides their lessons (rather than simply learning teacher-imposed ideas or techniques). Finally, teachers who are more curious and engaged themselves have students who are more curious and engaged in kind.

Allow Autonomous and Effortless Learning

The aid we have from others is mechanical,
compared with the discoveries of nature in us.
What is thus learned is delightful in the doing,
and the effect remains.

—Ralph Waldo Emerson

As he walked to his office in Delhi, Indian educator and researcher Sugata Mitra usually saw children playing in the slum. They were too poor to attend school but nevertheless were filled with energy and a hunger for knowledge. He lamented the lack of funding for public schools, to say nothing about the skills these children would need to thrive in today's global civic society and economy. There certainly would not be enough funds to provide computers for these children, never mind the money to hire trained computer teachers. Then it hit him: Children throughout time have learned the skills they have needed to survive. Learning always finds a way.

Mitra decided to simply give the children a computer, and see what they would do with it.

In a place where few had ever had the opportunity to see or use such technology, Mitra cut a hole in the wall outside his office and installed a new computer with Internet access. On the very day the station was set up, the children of the neighborhood (many of whom had no formal education at all) came over to check it out and play with it. There was no instructor on call; they were completely left to themselves. Astonishingly, within five hours, these children were surfing websites, downloading films, and using graphic software. When Mitra stopped by to check in, the children reassured him that things were going fine, but there was just one problem: they needed a faster processor! In fact, within days of setting up the hole-in-the-wall computer, local children of all ages had learned how to use virtually all of the common functions on a PC, such as cut and paste, drag and drop, and how to rename and save files (Mitra, 2006). Since then, Mitra and his colleagues have installed hole-in-the-wall computers throughout the developing world and found similar results, serving as a reminder of just how powerful and robust learning can be (Mitra, 2007). Given enough wonder and interest, learners can rapidly and completely understand complex content and skills entirely on their own.

As we see so clearly in the hole-in-the-wall experiments, humans come into this world curious, motivated, and ready to learn. They have an astounding capacity to respond to novelty and pick up information. Cognitive and developmental scientists have spent the last two decades trying to understand the ease with which infants and children learn new and fundamental skills. In fact, children pick up even the most challenging abilities autonomously and effortlessly. Because learners come with highly structured biology and highly structured social and cultural contexts, they are able to usher themselves into new learning (Romberg & Saffran, 2010).

Perhaps the most profound example of autonomous and effortless learning is coming to understand and speak one's native language. As a graduate student, I spent my days testing infants in the Infant Speech Perception Laboratory at Virginia Tech. New parents would come into our lab raving about the intellectual feats that their 10-month-olds had accomplished—convinced that these precocious achievements could not possibly be in the range of normal. My colleagues and I used to joke that all parents thought their infants are geniuses. In a way, they were spot on: When it comes to learning language, babies *are* geniuses. They easily become experts in understanding and producing language, which is far from easy to learn.

Understanding and speaking a native language is arguably the most complicated thing we will ever learn in our lives. It involves remembering and correctly using approximately 80,000 words and phrases. This includes knowing the sounds that are used in one's native language, plus remembering the rules for combining sounds sequentially in order to form words. Finally, learning language requires understanding a set of meanings for those words, the rules for combining these words into sentences, and the rules for relating sentences to larger meanings (Saffran, 2003). Children master these skills fully by the age of 2 or 3, with practically zero instruction. (We never hear a parent say, "Put an 'ing' on that verb, honey, if you want to make it into a present participle!") Simply by being around others using language, children are able to glean all of the complex rules of their native grammar. Research has shown that babies extract patterns of the structure of their native language using probabilities (Romberg & Saffran, 2010). Of course, infants are completely unaware that they are using statistics to learn how to talk—this, too, just comes naturally to them. It is no wonder that language has been described as the "crowning glory" of the human species. Children learn language efficiently and without error. Their learning is so facile that most of the time we are completely unaware of it—until the child unexpectedly says something so fluent that we ask ourselves, "Where on earth did she learn to say that?" (Smith, 2003, p. 256). Just like the results of Mitra's hole-in-the-wall experiments, language learning provides resounding evidence that children can learn autonomously and effortlessly.

Beyond infancy, self-directed learning remains a fact of life. Children learn because they find grappling with ideas fascinating and because it gives order and unity to their world. In one powerful study, elementary students were given a variety of different liquids and encouraged to experiment with them to figure out which ones, when mixed together, would bubble (Kuhn & Ho, 1980). The researchers watched closely to observe the process that students used to test out the various liquids. In fact, the children quickly and easily learned the intended principle (that manipulating one variable at a time is the best way to conduct a scientific experiment) completely on their own when they were allowed to try things out, follow their own intuitions, and make mistakes. When driven by curiosity instead of a script, they not only remained on task, they accomplished the learning goals independently.

Of course, reverence for children's bottom-up, natural ability to learn is not new. It has simply gone out of fashion, as our schools have become more focused on quantifiable results. In his seminal text *Emile: Or on Education* (1762/1979), philosopher Jean-Jacques Rousseau stressed the importance of granting the child freedom to grow and learn without being imposed upon. He believed that children's natural curiosity and independence was stifled by society and that the best learning was via direct, active exploration and experience. To Rousseau, a child put in a Robinson Crusoe–type experience would prosper. Learning to survive on a secluded island (much like learning how to use a computer through a hole in the wall) would lead the child to the exploration and active engagement that underpins discovery.

Throughout human history, parents and teachers have been relying on children's inherent and effortless capacity to learn. In hunter-gatherer cultures (from which all of our ancestors came), it is widely accepted that children educate themselves via self-directed exploration and play. They have done this for centuries, and it is hard to argue with the results (Gray, 2013). Even though adults in cultures such as the !Kung of the Kalahari Desert in South Africa, the Batek of Malaysia, or the Tauripans in Venezuela do not try to motivate, control, or direct their children's learning in any way, the children learn virtually all of the physical and cognitive skills they need to thrive. Children learn skills such as animal tracking and hunting, designing and building homes, cooking, and playing instruments by watching, imitating, spending time with peers and adults, playing organized games, and playing freely (Gray, 2013). In the case of the Aka and Bofi of Congo, young children—and even infants—are simply given the tools they will need and set free to figure them out. "Parents make small axes, digging sticks, baskets and spears for infants and young children. These are small-sized artifacts that reflect the size of the infant or child and are not toys. Mothers place these implements in their baskets and while resting on a net hunt or other subsistence activity, they will be given to infants. The infants chop, dig, etc." (Hewlett, Fouts, Boyette, & Hewlett, 2011, p. 1174). Anthropologists have used the term "osmosis" to refer to the ease with which hunter-gatherer children in small social groups acquire such intricate knowledge and skills without any teaching at all. It is seemingly automatic, with all children gaining proficiency (Gaskins & Paradise, 2010).

The same sort of osmosis learning is also common here in the United States within alternative school and unschooling communities. Students can learn complex "school skills"—like reading, writing, and math—in the absence of any formal curriculum. This does not mean that children learn without the help of others. Quite the contrary. Just like learning to speak or learning to use a computer in a hole in the wall, children can and do learn to read, write, think, and do math by joining communities of learners. To illustrate, at the Summerhill School in the United Kingdom (whose motto is "Founded in 1921. Still ahead of its time."), all lessons are voluntary, and formal curriculum is never delivered, yet students emerge as literate, thoughtful members of society. Why do they learn? Because children are exquisite, superb learners. How do they learn? By allowing their natural curiosity to flourish and by allowing them to join active, engaged communities of learners.

In a more local example, at the Sudbury Valley School in Massachusetts, children are given zero reading curriculum or formal lessons on how to read throughout their K–12 experience, and yet 100 percent of Sudbury Valley School students graduate literate, and have for nearly 50 years. The students there learn to read, write, do math, articulate, and think critically in all different timeframes and styles, but they do so in the same way that children all over the world learn to speak—that is, by community-joining (Ostroff, 2012). In a recent study, psychologist Peter Gray and his colleagues documented the process of how students learned to read without being formally taught at the Sudbury Valley School. The study showed that there was an incredible range in both the time it took to read and the path that children followed—with some students reading fluently within weeks of beginning and other students taking years. A few of the children in the study had learned consciously and deliberately (by studying phonics or grammar), but more commonly, students said that they just "picked it up." In many cases, individuals just realized one day that they could read, but neither they nor their parents or teachers had any idea how they had learned it. Said one mom of an unschooled child, "I watched my 5-year-old daughter teach herself to read and write. It was the most amazing thing to watch. It was like she was a code breaker" (Gray, 2012).

Effortless reading fits well into the framework of developmental psychologist Lev Vygotsky, who believed that children first gain new skills socially, in collaboration with more advanced peers. According to Vygotsky (1934/1998), only later do children begin to use those skills on their own and for their own purposes. The enterprise of learning should be totally effortless in order to be worthwhile. The minute the child is bored with one thing, he must be free to move to another thing. Only then will he discover the gold that is undirected trial-and-error-based research (Taleb, 2012). We can trust in the overwhelming research on the resilience of children's learning, and give children back their childhood as a time of curiosity and exploration.

Quick Recap

- ▶ Humans are exquisite learners.
- ▶ Children can learn effortlessly and on their own, given the right social conditions.
- ▶ Children can learn such complex skills as speaking, reading, using computers, and using tools without any formal instruction.
- ▶ Effortless learning occurs when children work with more advanced peers and when they join communities of learners.
- ▶ Teachers can trust curiosity to guide children to learning.

Unstructure the Schedule

Effortless learning can only emerge when children are given the time to explore and experiment. Unstructured time in the day is crucial for learning and success, even within more conventional school settings. In particular, recent research has shown that unstructuring the schedule is critical for the development of executive functions.

To do well in their daily lives, and especially to thrive in school, children need to learn to control their thoughts and feelings and their bodies.

Executive functions are those cognitive skills that children use to regulate their thoughts and actions toward specific goal-directed behaviors. They include focusing, planning and making appropriate choices, and transitioning well from one task to another. Performing well on tests of executive functioning is the number one predictor of how likely a child is to succeed in school from kindergarten all the way through high school graduation (Best, Miller, & Naglieri, 2011; Blair & Razza, 2007; Cameron et al., 2012).

When my kids listen to me and brush their teeth right away in the morning, getting out the door to school is so much more pleasant. Inhibiting their desire to continue playing and instead do what their mother asks them to do exercises executive functioning. But the most highly developed form of executive functioning is self-directed executive functioning, in which children are not merely able to follow the plan laid out by the teacher or parent, but able to make their own plans. Just imagine how easy our morning would be if Alexei and Sonia just went in and brushed their teeth on their own! (In my fantasy version of our mornings, they say to themselves, "First I'll brush my teeth, and then I'll get dressed and tell Mom that I'm ready for school.") Developing self-directed executive function is a key part of growing up, and not only is it helpful in getting out the door, it also pays dividends when it comes to doing well in school.

In a new and important study, researchers looked at the development of executive functioning in elementary school children. They examined the amount of time that children spent in structured versus unstructured activities outside of the classroom, and whether that affected how these kids did on tests of executive functioning. Structured activities included things like soccer practice, piano lessons, and homework. Unstructured activities were anything that the children chose on their own, including free play alone and with friends, playing board games or computer games, reading, hiking, climbing, or riding bikes. Results showed that the more time children spent in unstructured activities, the better they did on tests of self-directed executive function. The inverse was also true. Children whose free time was highly scheduled performed more poorly on self-directed executive function tasks across the board (Barker et al., 2014).

Unstructured blocks of time give children an opportunity to plan and practice self-control. Providing too much structure deprives the children of the learning opportunity of discovering how to regulate their behavior on their own. One key way that we can promote effortless and autonomous learning in the classroom (and to allow children's curiosity to persist and flourish) is by providing unstructured time on the schedule.

Curiosity Technique to Try: Unstructuring Time

There are often opportunities for unstructured time during transitions to new lessons or projects. Have you ever noticed that your students want to play around and act up in those in-between times? I remember being a student and relishing those few in-between moments as an opportunity to explore or check out the materials for the next lesson in my own way. I just wanted to test out the xylophone before the music class began or flip ahead in the math workbook to see what was coming up next. A chance to check out the microscopes and look at whatever I wanted—fabric from my sweater, skin from a scab—would have been so satisfying. For some reason, these mini-attempts at curiosity were always thwarted by my teachers. Were they afraid that I would not be able to get back on task? In fact, the research on attention shows the opposite—we need mini brain breaks in attention in order to sustain focus (Ostroff, 2014). In any case, the message was clear: in the name of control, I was supposed to squelch my natural urge for exploring.

Second grade teacher Leticia Jenkins recently admitted that the math manipulatives sit in the closet of her classroom. Her school has not yet integrated them into the school's math lesson planning, and she was told to keep them out of harm's way. But math manipulatives are meant to be explored by small hands with big ideas. Learning is a hands-on enterprise, and unstructured learning offers a boon to curiosity. The next time you need to switch gears in your classroom, try scheduling in some unstructured time. Since we know that unstructured playing time is the number one way children learn, let them play with the classroom materials. Mitra had to trust that the students in the slums of Delhi would not vandalize or destroy the computers in the holes in the wall. Likewise, if we entrust children with the autonomy to create their own classroom rules concerning equipment handling, and give them some unstructured time, we will be offering them experience with executive functioning tools that they need to succeed in school and in life.

The simplest and most obvious way to provide unstructured time during the school day is to protect and preserve recess. Arguably the best learning experience of the day—the place where children are left alone to explore and experiment—is free play at recess. Children learn most of the skills that they will need to be effective in the classroom and in life via play, which they automatically do and cannot be stopped from doing. During free play a child is given the opportunity to master new competencies and integrate existing knowledge via manipulating, exploring, discovering, and practicing, all without the burden of external goals or rules (Bruce, 1991).

When my dad was in elementary school in the 1950s, he spent three hours per day outside in unstructured (executive function boosting) free play: that is, at recess. Half of his day was spent working out this own rules, governing his thoughts and his feelings and his body in concert with his peers, inventing games in real time, exercising self-control, negotiating issues of justice and injustice, and being physically active. This was all done in the absence of adult intervention. Today we are fighting an absurd fight to hold onto the portion of the school day that may just be the healthiest and most beneficial to children. It is estimated that up to 30 percent of schools do not even have recess anymore (Holmes, Pellegrini, & Schmidt, 2006). By limiting or eliminating recess, some educators believe that they are providing children more opportunities to learn, when in fact they are doing quite the opposite. Structuring children's time with so-called "enrichment" or "academic" time instead of letting them be free at recess reflects a profound misunderstanding of how young children learn (Kohn, 2015).

Curiosity Technique to Try: Kidwatching

Educators Jean Anne Clyde and Mark Condon (2000) have claimed that teachers must observe students in naturalistic settings to truly appreciate what sophisticated learners they are. They recall an experience in a museum:

> We entered a cave like exhibit where hundreds of fascinating stones, minerals, and glittering crystals were displayed . . .

before long we found ourselves behind two young boys, about 8 and 9. Because they were so intensely focused on their investigation of the exhibit, they were unaware of our presence. We, however, were completely captivated by theirs. We were struck by the sophistication of their questions to each other and remarks to themselves regarding what they were seeing and experiencing . . . we were particularly impressed with the seriousness of the boys' investigation. . . . No adults were there to direct them, yet they were so engaged—so driven to find answers to their own questions. (Clyde & Condon, 2000, p. 2).

In her groundbreaking 1978 article, education professor Yetta Goodman suggested that the best form of learning assessment is "kidwatching," which is the informal and direct observation of children in a variety of naturalistic situations. To try kidwatching during school, just open up part of the day (even just a short block of time at first) to free play. Free play simply emerges from unstructured timeframes, so it is for all students, not just for young children. No matter how you set up the situation, children will begin to explore in, make sense of, and have fun in the time and space you allow them.

Let yourself observe and wonder about the things they do or say. Position yourself as a researcher of childhood behavior, and note what you discover. Remember, all experiences are learning experiences. When does Julio have the most energy? What is Emil trying to do over there? Jasmine is so focused on her sketches. What is she learning from them? Nicki is teasing Rebecca. Why is she feeling the need to harness power? Is she feeling powerless in other ways? Your hypotheses will bring you closer to understanding your students as learners who are always learning. After one of these free periods, ask yourself, "What can I do to help them and to scaffold the connections that they are already making?" (Clyde & Condon, 2000). Finish this sentence for each of your students: "Julio is curious about _____," "Emil is curious about _____," and "Jasmine is curious about _____."

This can also be done with middle or high school students, during an autonomous seminar discussion, lab, or group project. While the students are freely working, step outside of the role of teacher for a few minutes and observe them. What types of questions is each student asking? Who is emerging as a facilitator or leader? What motives are guiding each student's behavior? Over the course of a week, answer questions like the following about each of your students: "Rachel is interested in_____," Darnell is motivated by _____," or "Mariana is hoping for _____."

For another perspective, combine classes with a colleague and let the big group spend unstructured time together. Watch the students from the other class. What do you notice about them? What can your colleague tell you about your students? Exchange lists and challenge each other to finish the statement, "Nicki is curious about_____" for one another's students. Compare answers and see whether you and your colleague observed similar characteristics during your kidwatch.

Provide Choices

In Ms. Ling's kindergarten class, the children arrive and take a few minutes to settle into the new day. They put their things away, chat with their friends, and look around at the new materials that have been put out for centers. They then sit in circle, where they sing songs, talk about the jobs for the day, and do the morning rituals like calendar and weather. When it is time for centers, the children choose which table to sit or stand at, get a brief lesson about the materials and their potential uses, and then decide how they will spend their time. Some children spend the entire centers time at one table, working hard on the art project, solving problems with the math materials, or preparing a snack at the cooking table. Some spend only a few minutes at each place, but then double back to complete what they had started. Others, who may be in a quiet mood, sit quietly in the reading corner. Ms. Ling and her assistant teachers float around the room offering ideas for extending the children's ideas at the art table, helping when someone is stuck on a math problem or checking in on the snack production. Children in Ms. Ling's class tend to spend over an hour in centers. There is talking and movement and laughing, but the overall classroom has a feeling of peace. Ms. Ling experiences very few behavior problems.

In Ms. D'Amato's kindergarten class, the students come in and put their things away quietly. They then sit in circle for 30–40 minutes listening or sharing with their peers. They too sing songs and decide on the daily jobs; they talk about the calendar and the weather. They too go to centers to do art projects or work on spelling. But when circle time is over and they head to centers, they look to find where their name cards have been placed (they are assigned seats to keep things less confusing). For artwork, there is an example to model, and following directions is rewarded. The children trace the patterns for the body and wings of the owl on construction paper, glue them in place, and then glue on the eyes and feathers. When they have done all three, they are allowed to sit quietly in their chairs and wait for the bell, which signals it's time to clean up and move on. Most kids are done quickly, so Ms. D'Amato has shortened centers time to 20 minutes. She does not want idle children fooling around. The rules are tighter because Ms. D'Amato believes that well-behaved children will learn better, but the children are not better behaved. Often, Ms. D'Amato's students complain of boredom, and she is wondering what she can structure in for the kids who have finished their owls in five minutes or less (Grossman, 2008). Like Ms. D'Amato, teachers who believe that they are providing good boundaries for children are sometimes inadvertently giving the wrong messages.

When children are given too many restrictions and not enough choices, their motivation becomes quickly depleted, they feel that their independence has been stifled, and they begin to feel resentful or want to rebel. If children are not allowed to choose, or if their choices are very limited, they will not develop the skills to approach problems or to stretch their minds to think of things in new ways. When children are told exactly how to do every step of a project or problem, they begin to feel that originality is misbehavior and exploration is a waste of time. Telling children exactly what they should be doing and how they should do it encourages them to simply follow directions by rote. Their curiosity and exploration will both promptly shut down. If choice provokes interest, and interest primes achievement, then it's not much of a stretch to suggest that the learning environments in which students get to make decisions about what they're doing will be the most effective (Anderson, 2016). Research shows us that autonomous students are, almost across the board, curious and intrinsically motivated (Fazey & Fazey, 2001). Yet, in most learning environments, kids spend the majority of their time just following directions (Kohn, 2011).

Give Students a Real Voice in Their Own Learning

Study hard what interests you the most in the most undisciplined, irreverent, and original manner possible.

—Richard Feynman, Perfectly Reasonable Deviations from the Beaten Track

All humans need to feel that they are exercising choice over their lives. This is an evolutionary adaptation linked to survival. When a situation spirals out of our control and we find ourselves without choices, our biochemistry is quickly altered, shutting down the higher thinking centers of the brain and shifting us into fight or flight mode. On the flip side, autonomy is one of the most pleasurable experiences for a developing child. For evidence, merely look on the face of an infant who has just learned to reach and grasp something or one who has just learned to crawl. Likewise, look at the faces of the children as they run out the door to recess. When children are given the opportunity to take control of their lives or their learning—to choose in the classroom—they develop self-motivation and a sense of responsibility.

In a curiosity classroom, teachers plan for a range of tasks, both those that are teacher-initiated and those that are child-initiated (Fisher, 2013). Children are allowed freedom to move on to the next task when they have successfully completed the previous one, just as Ms. Ling's kindergarten class is run. When children are allowed to make choices, they practice regulating and controlling their minds and bodies (all prerequisites for executive functioning). They feel empowered and therefore have no need to break rules behind the teacher's back or exert power over others. This is especially true as children get older and into the middle and high school years. These students need to direct and manage their own academic repertoire in order to feel actively engaged and sustainably motivated. "The wise teacher understands that children make choices all day long, whether adults want them to or not. They choose to obey, ignore, or defy rules and directions and determine for themselves whether to speak kindly or angrily to others. They decide whether school or child care is a good place to be" (Grossman, 2008).

Children are more highly motivated to participate in activities they have chosen for themselves. They are also more actively engaged (Reeve, Nix, & Hamm, 2003). And research has shown that the opportunity to make meaningful academic choices is directly related to students' success in classroom work (d'Ailly, 2003; McCombs, 2015). In one study, when 2nd graders were given the chance to decide which tasks they would work on at any given moment, their engagement skyrocketed—and they completed significantly more learning tasks in far less time (Wang & Stiles, 1976).

One way that student choice can be achieved is by differentiated instruction, which involves tweaking the lesson in small but important ways to take into account the strengths and challenges of the individual learner. In addition to changes based on ability, instruction can also be differentiated by student interest.

> If Mr. Purdy, for example, wants all of his children to learn some important concepts about weather, he can offer a variety of activities. Some children will learn by observing the water cycle in a terrarium, others will learn from fiction and nonfiction books, and others will explore their personal experiences with weather by using paints and expressive materials. Each child will learn in his or her own way, but all will learn about weather. (Grossman, 2008)

Teachers sometimes fear that they will lose control over their classroom if they leave too many choices up to the students. In fact, research shows just the opposite. When children feel a sense of agency regarding their thoughts and feelings and actions, they are much more likely to take responsibility for the learning situation (d'Ailly, 2003, 2004). For this reason, every single school day must include at least one block of time in which students decide individually what to do. Free reading, journaling, and creative writing are all good beginnings, as is letting students choose their mode of response to a text or topic. A poem or play, sculpture or video, drawing or comic panel can be equally challenging and effective (Kohn, 1993).

In a large Colorado middle school, there was a gang of tough students that even the teachers were afraid of. They were reportedly unreachable and epically unmotivated. Research psychologist Barbara McCombs made it her project to understand these students and what was driving their behavior. She began by inconspicuously following them around throughout their school day, sitting in the back of the room during each of their class periods. What she observed was that while this gang of students disrupted, tuned out, and even started fights in some classes, there was one class in which all of them behaved, participated, and cooperated. McCombs was astounded to discover that it was a math class at the end of a long school day where this group of kids became self-disciplined and responsible. Upon entering the room, they quietly got their folders, paired up in groups, and began working on their projects without the slightest direction or command from the teacher. The teacher was in the room, but he was mostly in the back or going from group to group to check in and ask about their progress. He had set up an entirely self-controlled and self-directed learning environment and classroom culture. He trusted his students enough to allow them autonomy and self-control. When asked what his secret was, the teacher simply explained that he believed all students, even those who have been labeled disruptive, have a natural desire to learn. He had told his math class on the first day, "This is your class . . . we can do it any way you want as long as you learn the math" (McCombs, 2015). He did lay out some nonnegotiables—the essential pieces necessary to cover content standards and to ensure that the work got done—but beyond that, he left the options and details up to the students. By entering into a spoken contract, this middle school math teacher had earned the respect of even the "difficult" kids. The classroom community set the rules and enforced those rules between one another. This made the teacher's job exponentially easier and more enjoyable—and all of his energy and passion could be funneled back into the learning situation (McCombs, 2015).

Quick Recap

▶ Too few choices can harm children's motivation.

▶ Choosing is an evolutionary adaptation linked to survival.

▶ For a learning environment to be effective, students need to make daily decisions about what they do and how they spend their time.

Curiosity Technique to Try:
Student-Designed Pedagogy and Curriculum

. . . two words: Trust Children. Nothing could be more simple—
or more difficult. Difficult, because to trust children we must first
learn to trust ourselves—and most of us were taught as children
that we could not be trusted.

—John Holt, *How Children Learn*

Veteran 5th grade teacher Richard Lauricella says he would have burned out decades ago if not for the fact that he involves his students in designing the curriculum. At the beginning of a new unit, Mr. Lauricella says to his students, "What's the most exciting way we could study this?" If individuals or groups suggest something that isn't feasible, he will say, "Okay, what's the next most exciting way we could study this?" (Lickona, 1991, p. 148). The students always come up with good proposals, and they are motivated because he's using their ideas. As a result, the 5th graders never do the unit in the same way twice. This doesn't just motivate the curiosity of the students, it allows Mr. Lauricella to learn new things, too.

Another way to appeal to student interest and curiosity is by introducing the unfamiliar through the familiar. You can use students' current knowledge, interests, and experiences with a familiar concept to bridge to a novel one. If your students are interested in a particular videogame, for example, you might bridge to the background mathematics and programming that allows the game to work. Students might then be given a choice about designing a particular game routine related to these concepts. When students have the opportunity to be involved in the lesson from the ground up, they will take ownership of the learning process. The lines will suddenly blur between what they do for work and what they do for pleasure.

In a course I teach called The Biased Brain, we spend a semester examining how the human brain, in its exquisite pattern seeking and anticipating, fills in gaps in our perception and leaves us open to being duped. When I first was designing the class, I wanted to give the students a role in running it. I picked topics and readings that I found fascinating for each week of the course (things like hallucinations, subliminal messages, sleight of hand/

magic, false memories, and synesthesia) and let pairs of students facilitate the seminar on them. Whereas I thought I was giving students control in the course design, the results were rather disappointing—they still were doing my work on my interests.

The next time I taught the course, I took a leap of faith in my students and handed them over the control of both the content and method. For the first 4 weeks, I chose foundational readings to set the stage. Then, as a class, we brainstormed topics and ideas that were interesting to all of us. We negotiated and voted and laid out the topics for the next 11 weeks of the semester. After that, student pairs each selected a week that would belong completely to them. They provided the readings for the group, facilitated the discussion on them, conducted in-class activities and experiences, and offered feedback to their peers on their papers. The switch was astounding—in version number two, my students were enthusiastic and engaged, held each other to high standards, and brought incredibly creative insights and activities to our sessions. They also learned the material more deeply, as I observed from their final research papers. It took my letting go to give them a chance to fully step in.

Curiosity Technique to Try: Conduct an Action Research Project

An action research project ties learning to students' current passions and interests. It also hooks them into civic engagement within their community. To begin an action research project, first, brainstorm together what needs to be done. What do they care about? Make a list of priorities. Perhaps there is an unsafe intersection where students cross to get to school or a park that needs to be cleaned up. Maybe the lunch block is too rushed or the students do not feel that they have enough choices for special periods. Next, create objectives in line with curriculum standards, plus individual and collective student interests and choices. In small-group discussions, students can hash out personal preferences and then see how these fit with the more general class list. What do the students want to do? Third, form teams and hit the pavement. Students will need to draft action plans. They may need to write reports and letters addressed to the principal, school board, or city.

One summer, a group of high school math students in Philadelphia were sitting in summer school sweating and complaining. The high temperatures made doing math almost impossible. But then their clever teacher had an idea. She decided to turn all that impassioned argument about the need for air conditioning into an action research project. The students began investigating air conditioning systems, calculating the number of units that their school building would need based on its size and layout, estimating costs and getting bids, and drafting a proposal to the town. In the process, the students learned about things like systems of equations and slope, with the added bonus of learning how to be engaged classroom participants and citizens (Schwartz, 2014a).

Let Students Self-Assess

One powerful way of providing autonomy to your students is to let them choose how to demonstrate mastery of a concept. You can structure in ways for students to assess their own learning progress by using charts or keeping journals, so they can evaluate how they have changed as they acquire relevant knowledge and skills. As students learn to monitor themselves, they become more motivated by their successes and begin to acquire a sense of ownership and responsibility for the role they play in these successes. It's relatively straightforward to create a format for them to self-monitor their comprehension of the content and reflect upon their process of learning.

Before handing in any formal written work, I often ask my students to turn over their papers and list three strengths and three things that need more work. In this same vein, to begin self-assessment, students might develop the criteria on which they will be assessing. Have them brainstorm what a top-notch exemplar of this assignment would look like. Then they may request the kind of feedback they would like from the teacher when they hand in work, in relation to the criteria they have themselves generated. Another option includes compiling selected work for a portfolio (with commentary on why they have chosen what they have to represent their learning).

Curiosity Technique to Try: Main Lesson Books and Electronic Portfolios

In the Waldorf education model, from the philosophy of Austrian pedagogue Rudolf Steiner, students represent what they have learned within each academic unit in carefully crafted notebooks called main lesson books. Students put time, care, and great depth into the process of creatively capturing their lesson content from their own individual perspective. They also integrate their understanding across interdisciplinary topics. The goal is for the student to create something, but also to slow down and work with care, form letters and figures beautifully, and develop a sense for the aesthetic (Simmons, 2009). For students, these blank books become almost sacred texts throughout their school year, chronicling their journey of discovery as much as the new information and knowledge itself. For botany, for example, a child might make a book that includes sketches, leaf pressings, poems, graphs, photos, and paintings. At parents' meetings and public events, teachers often collect a selection of the class books, and students get to take pride in showcasing their individual work. At the end of the year, students carefully carry the main lesson books home and use them even years later to refer back to the big picture of what they learned (Simmons, 2009). Like writing their own textbooks, these students find the intersection of the objective material with the personal experience.

More recently, high schools, colleges, and universities began asking students to compile and showcase their learning across the curriculum in electronic portfolios. Like a main lesson book, an e-portfolio gives content and the learning process equal import. I am currently teaching a capstone course in which students assess their own learning using artifacts and work samples they have collected in an e-portfolio. My students tell me that this is a transformative journey that is almost endlessly engaging. Using e-portfolios, students can revisit their work over time and look for greater meanings and patterns. They are captains of their own learning journeys, and are in awe of what they have accomplished. These models of representation and self-reflection are ideal for formative assessment and can be used at any age.

Let Students Work Together

Working together in groups is how humans have always learned. When it comes to fostering effortless learning without the surveillance of teachers, working with friends is a surefire strategy. The work quickly transforms into something social, or a game. In short, learning together is fun. Much of the effortless learning of children happens because kids feel that they are part of social clubs or communities. Education philosopher Frank Smith (2003) believes that most of the learning we do is the effortless byproduct of joining clubs. When you become part of something bigger than yourself, you suddenly get the benefit of identifying with other members. When babies are surrounded by people using language, they learn it quickly and efficiently—but not because they are setting out to achieve something cognitive. On the contrary, people learn it because of the company they keep or the communities they want to join. When you join a club (like the speaking language club), you immediately get the sense, "You are one of us" or "I am just like you." New activities, with their associated knowledge and expectations, are suddenly available to you and other members will help you do the things that interest you. You learn without realizing it.

When teacher Leah Amaru and her colleagues noticed how effortlessly and effectively kindergartners and 5th graders worked together, they decided to extend buddy time to include content lessons for both groups.

> During buddy activities, my colleague and I started to notice that these 5th graders were becoming overly excited about drawing and coloring. These 10-year-old children needed more kid-friendly events in their lives (not more multiple choice tests and essay writing lessons). So we began planning content lessons on literacy, social studies, or science for them to complete together. During one project (creating a map of our town), it was the kindergartners who were more experienced and prepared, so they took the lead! It was amazing to see children five years apart working collaboratively. They were upset when it was time to stop, so we spent three more days adding details and working on planning techniques, social and

leadership skills, oral language, fine motor skills, and spelling. (Leah Amaru, personal communication, April 6, 2015)

We also now have resounding evidence that collaboration catapults learning. This is because students can merge their own understanding and insights with that of a partner. In the brain, thanks to mirror neurons, doing something oneself is no different from watching a peer do something you are intent on. Furthermore, working with peers who are a bit more experienced can bootstrap learners into more complex territory very efficiently. As developmental scientist Lev Vygotsky (1967/2004) always said, what you can do today only with the help of more advanced peers, you can do tomorrow on your own.

When working in groups, students take turns being managers of conversations, thereby learning to be good coaches, empowering others, and expressing personal interest in team members. Working together, students begin to help their team achieve well-being and successes. Collaborating requires being a good communicator and listener, identifying and implementing a clear vision and strategy for the team (Wiggins, 2013). As students progress from elementary grades through middle and high school, their abilities to be good collaborators and to lead effective inquiry teams becomes increasingly important. Because of our technology-based economy and the value of innovation, collaborating is rapidly becoming one of the main goals of 21st century upper level schooling.

Curiosity Technique to Try: Collaborative, Real-Time Technology

There are emerging technologies appropriate to students across the age span, which can stimulate creative collaboration and learner-centered dialogue. For example, TodaysMeet is a chat room that allows students to communicate with one another and the larger group in real time during classroom lessons. By posting to TodaysMeet, students get their ideas heard, and the backchannel conversation—the social realm of learning—is brought to the forefront. TodaysMeet can be used for drawing out comments from the students (even the shyest students) during a lesson. It can be used to share links to a website you want your class to check out. During a lecture or presentation or film, kids can ask quick questions using TodaysMeet without interrupting. Students can also give examples of how something relates to their lives—just post them and everyone can see immediately, which is much quicker than raising hands. Likewise, you can take a quick poll with everyone weighing in and discovering the dynamics of the group—give a few choices, and within minutes the results will be visible to the entire group. You can ask comprehension questions or gather feedback, anonymously if you want ("How can we change the process of presenting so that every member of the group participates evenly?"). You can even write collaborative poems or stories. Just start a TodaysMeet chat room with a story starter, and have each student successively add to it (Miller, 2014).

Curiosity Technique to Try: Collaborative Exams

At Stanford University, a handful of psychology professors do something simple but revolutionary: they give exams in pairs. Professor Philip Zimbardo began by teaching two sections of Introduction to Psychology. The two sections used identical material, curriculum, and pedagogy; the only difference was that one group took the exams in pairs. The results were astonishing: students who took tests together performed significantly better on all exams throughout the course, and their scores were more consistent over time. Collaborative test takers also reported a host of positive attitudes, including reduced test anxiety and higher confidence. Collaborating let them enjoy the course more, and learn effortlessly. They even reported more interest toward the topic of psychology in general (Zimbardo, Butler, & Wolfe, 2003).

There are many ways we can loosen up the assessment situation and let students work together. Students can study together, self-assess on their levels of preparation, and come to understand each other's strengths. On test day students can quietly whisper strategies to each other or work silently on problems and then review the steps together. Removing the stress of the testing situation, and letting kids work the way kids have always worked—collaboratively—can encourage learners to open up, be curious, and enjoy the process.

Quick Recap

▶ When students design the topics or method of learning, they become more curious and engaged.

▶ Action research is a powerful technique for both curiosity and civic engagement.

▶ Self-assessment makes the learning process more meaningful for students.

▶ Collaboration catapults learning.

▶ Even collaborative exams allow learners to open up, be curious, and enjoy learning.

In Sum

We can relax in knowing that infants and children can learn incredibly complex skills (like talking, using tools, and reading) with ease and without direct instruction. When driven by curiosity, learners explore and find patterns they need to crack the codes of intricate knowledge and ideas. They are able to do this thanks to the biological systems they come into the world with, and thanks to the highly predictable nature of their social and cultural surround.

Free and unstructured time is crucial for autonomous learning to occur. Unstructured time gives children the opportunity to learn planning and self-control, hallmarks of executive functioning that are strongly associated with success in school. Recess time (at risk in packed school day schedules) is one of the most beneficial parts of the school day for learning, since it is unstructured by definition. We must protect our students' natural abilities to engage and learn effortlessly by giving them choices in planning their school work, both for content and process.

Embrace Intrinsic Motivation

Do not follow the ideas of others, but learn to listen to the voice within yourself.

—Dogen Zenji

In the Looney Tunes short animated film *One Froggy Evening*, a construction worker unearths a little frog from the cornerstone of a demolished building. Upon being pulled out, the little frog jumps up, grabs a top hat and cane, and lunges his cartoon body into an old-timey high kick dance and song, "Hello my baby, hello my honey, hello my ragtime gal." Our hero sees dollar signs and begins trying to exploit Michigan J. Frog's talents for money. But in a hilarious turn of events, every time someone else comes along to see him (a talent agent, an audience in the theater the hopeful entrepreneur has rented, or a police officer in the park), the frog just falls back down and croaks. No singing, no dancing. The hat and cane fall down flat.

The starry-eyed worker is beyond disappointed and desperate. No matter what he does, Michigan J. Frog sings and dances ecstatically for him and won't go beyond croaking for everyone else. This tale demonstrates that the most genuinely pleasant experiences (singing, dancing, or learning) are not for display. Students are not show ponies; their learning experience will sometimes look magnificent and sometimes look mundane, but it above all belongs to them, and it must, in order to be authentic.

Behavioral scientists have spent the past century trying to understand learning, and one thing is for sure: whether we are talking about 4th graders or high school juniors, without motivation there is no learning. Luckily for us, children arrive in this world endlessly motivated to learn. True motivation—the kind that makes us want to get up and sing and dance—comes from within. It cannot be manufactured in the service of outside recognition or reward. Psychologists call this *intrinsic motivation*. Intrinsically motivated actions drive us from a deep place. We cannot be stopped from wanting to do them because we have an innate need for competence and control in our environments (de Charms, 1968; Deci, 1975; White, 1959). In the words of pioneer 19th century developmental psychologist Edwin Kirkpatrick, "Just as a free laborer does a vast deal more work than the most closely watched slave, and does it with a pleasure and self-respect the slave can never feel, so does the child, working under the stimulus of interest, accomplish far more intellectually and morally than the uninterested urchin who slaved at his task under the watchful eye of the old-time teacher" (1903/2009, p. 175).

When the impetus for learning comes from outside rather than inside, the student's focus is concentrated on pleasing others (what my colleagues and I refer to as "playing the game of school"). It is a performance, involving students less in the learning process or activity itself and focusing them on the outcomes (getting correct answers to the questions posed by those in power, as it were). Unfortunately, formal schooling, with its due dates, assessments, grades, and subjectivity to teachers' and parents' approval, tends to undo intrinsic motivation. In this situation, learning is no longer an expression of curiosity and interest, and children learn far less. For example, when an assignment is stressful or boring, students are significantly less likely to understand or remember the content. If a child becomes disinterested in a whole set of academic tasks, then he or she is unlikely to benefit from doing them (Kohn, 2011).

On the other hand, when the motivation to learn comes from the inside, students' passion and engagement are almost limitless. A high school math teacher was doing a unit on the beauty of numbers and showed her students how to generate a golden spiral using Fibonacci numbers and graph paper. One of the students, Evan, asked how big it could get, and she asked the group what they thought. Another boy realized with delighted surprise that one could keep going indefinitely. The following week Evan showed up to class with a gigantic spiral that he had made at home with dozens of pieces of graph paper taped together. He inspired the group to make one even bigger, and that led to discussions about how to execute it accurately. That became a completely unexpected and wonderful project that lasted three months and was eventually displayed—the final product was more than 15 feet long! Later, the teacher learned from Evan's mother that he had a profound dyscalculia and had hated math up to that point.

Outside Judgments

In a classic study of intrinsic motivation, researchers at Stanford University promised children a "good player award" for working on an art project. The awarded children became less drawn to working with the art materials during later free-play sessions. Children who had done the art project because they wanted to continued on (Lepper, Greene, & Nisbett, 1973). A more recent meta-analysis (a comparison of the findings of 128 separate experiments) showed that young children's intrinsic motivation, confidence, and self-determination were undermined by external rewards for learning such as gold stars, honor rolls, and best student awards (Deci, Koestner, & Ryan, 2001). When an outside force imposes a reason for doing the project, the project can lose its draw for the learner. On the contrary, when an activity is intrinsically motivating, the reward is part and parcel of the act itself. In one study, education researchers looked at those features of the learning situation that helped 3rd and 4th graders remember passages that they had read. How interested the students were in the passages mattered most of all. The most interesting passages were up to 30 times more memorable than the most readable ones (Anderson, Shirley, Wilson, & Fielding, 1987).

Even praise (which we tend to think of as a hallmark of self-esteem and learning) can harm intrinsic motivation (Henderlong & Lepper, 2002). In one study, children who were consistently praised for their performance on word search puzzles quickly lost interest in completing them. Another group that received no evaluation, positive or negative, continued to work on the puzzles (Kast & Connor, 1988). Sometimes children who are over-praised learn to only choose those activities that will please their teachers or parents. While this may initially sound appealing to us as parents and educators, in the long run these children are much less likely to be innovative, creative, or self-directing. They learn to conform to only those behaviors that will bring success and continued praise, rather than to take intellectual risks or to experiment with new things (Gordon, 1989). According to education philosopher Alfie Kohn, "The most notable aspect of a positive judgment is not that it is positive but that it is a judgment" (1993, p. 102). When we feel judged, we begin to look outward. Suddenly we see the activity we are engaged in within a different framework, raising the stakes and making us self-conscious. We drop our proverbial hat and cane, and just begin to croak in the corner of the box.

Like praise, surveillance harms intrinsic motivation and, ultimately, curiosity. If children feel hovered over, they naturally begin to worry about how they are doing and take fewer risks. Likewise, competition and pressure can deprive children of the joy and pleasure of creativity. Bouts of trial and error suddenly become win-lose situations, and self-judgment takes over for experimentation. Setting expectations for children's performances depletes their confidence, pressuring them to both perform and conform. Innovation, again, goes almost immediately dormant (Amabile & Hennessy, 1992). Worrying is antithetical to curiosity. In its extreme form, anxiety can squash curiosity altogether. Indeed, children who grow up in unpredictable or abusive environments tend to be incurious at school. This is because survival takes up most of their cognitive resources, leaving few for playful exploration (Leslie, 2014).

Freedom and Intrinsic Motivation

Sincere wonder and interest, plus a degree of freedom, is the recipe for keeping students intrinsically motivated. Being free to revel in the capriciousness and seemingly frivolous aspects of motivation—such as idle curiosity and playful tinkering—is in fact a very important feature of human development (Silvia, 2001). At a preschool in Massachusetts, when children were allowed to select the materials they used for making a collage, their work was judged as significantly more creative than the work of children who used exactly the same materials but did not get to choose them (Amabile & Gitomer, 1984). In another study, researchers recorded and catalogued 8-year-olds' questioning behaviors as they completed a problem-solving task. The questions that the children came up with on their own were much more likely to lead to further inquiry than the questions asked by others. "The critical factor [in effective problem solving] was that what the children said and did came from themselves, as a personal question, not because somebody else suggested it. Even if someone else originally asked a question, it only became a genuine question for the students when they asked it themselves, i.e., when they saw the contradiction or the puzzle they did not see before and set out to explain it" (Cifone, 2013, p. 52). In a third study, when students were given ownership of the learning situation (i.e., able to make major choices about what they would learn, how they would approach the topics, and when), the students reported being overwhelmingly more satisfied and intrinsically motivated. Importantly, these students also showed superior academic performance (de Charms, 1976).

One kindergarten teacher asked her students to circle all of the "e"s in a sentence on the board. A clever student found an "e" in his name and also circled that one. The teacher capitalized on this intrinsically motivated diversion from the original plan and directed her students to look for "e"s anywhere in the classroom. Since the children were allowed to reinterpret the original activity based on their own interests, their engagement multiplied. Later, when it came time for the students to choose a reading-related activity to work on, they initiated an "e-hunt," and virtually every student became excited about participating. When the same teacher tried to assign letter-hunts in sub-sequent years, the enthusiasm was never as strong as it was when the children initiated it themselves (Nolen, 2001). In each of these research studies, as in countless classrooms across the world, students constructed knowledge more effectively when their own authentic desires and ideas drove their learning.

Power and Powerlessness

Children seem to be universally intrinsically motivated when they begin their learning journeys. We never hear of preschoolers with motivation problems. As they go through formal schooling, however, their intrinsic motivation is often diminished. When students are forced to follow someone else's rules, study somebody else's curriculum, and be judged under someone else's evalua-tion (Kohn, 1993), they tend to feel powerless, which leads to burnout and disin-terest. Also, when academic skills become divorced from the natural contexts and utility of learning them, and get more and more abstract like radians in calculus or parts of sentence structure in language, their meaning quickly can slip away (Bruner, 1966). Although it is common for students to ask, "Why do we need to know this?" or "Will this be on the test?" these are actually alarming questions that indicate learners are only trying to jump through the hoops we have set up for them. National programs like No Child Left Behind and Race to the Top have led to more standardized testing and more teacher-directed, didactic instruction (Kohn, 2015). If a student asks whether he needs to mem-orize something for a test, he is letting us know that he is lacking intrinsic motivation—essentially saying, "My love of learning has been kicked out of me . . . now all I want to know is whether I have to do it, and what you will give me if I do" (Kohn, 1999, p. 200).

We need to fight to protect curiosity in our classrooms. Part of that call to action is making sure we do not revert to what I call "student as enemy" situa-tions. When we separate kids who are talking to one another rather than work-ing quietly; when we surprise students with a quiz if they don't seem prepared; when we make test questions purposely confusing to try to trick them; when we mount weed-out courses with impossible expectations to get rid of those students who do not immediately understand the material on their own—we are harming students. As teachers, our job is to help them locate the difference between their best work and indifferent work, to search not for faults but for possibilities (McWilliams, 2003). In my first year of college, I signed up to take calculus. I had taken precalculus in high school and done quite well. I remember liking the class, or at least liking the teacher. He felt that I had a pretty good mind for math. But in my college-level calculus class, the material was assigned, not taught. My teacher was an engineering graduate student who mostly got mad when someone asked her a question. The message was that any problem understanding the material was our fault, not hers. We came to believe that narrative quite readily, even those of us who thought we were pretty good at math. I realized quickly that her goal was to draw out the knowledge in those elite students who already had it, not to teach the rest of us anything at all. I was her enemy, and I was weeded out of a natural science focus fairly quickly. One thing was for sure: I hated math.

Curiosity Technique to Try: Everything Is Interesting

In this exercise, students are challenged to find something—anything—to genuinely connect with on a given topic and present their findings to the class. The more absurd the topics, and the more boring they seem at first glance, the more exciting it is for students to make links and connections to it. First, let the students come up with a list of people, places, or things as potential topics. The topics can connect with the lesson you are working on. You could pick an event from history (the Boer War) or a geometry theorem (the partition postulate) or a literary device (circumlocution). Individual students or teams of students are then set free to make that topic interesting and present it in a thought-provoking way to the class. They can add silliness and humor

Quick Recap

▶ Without motivation, there is no learning.

▶ Children are bursting with intrinsic motivation.

▶ Intrinsic motivation can be undermined by even well-meaning outside influences like rewards, praise, or surveillance.

▶ Intrinsic motivation is difficult to maintain without some degree of freedom, control, and power.

and even take the audience on a train of thought that has very little to do with the original topic, as long as they bring it back around to the original somehow. Think of it as an exercise in linking to new ideas. This exercise shows students that as interesting people, they can always find something to connect to in any discipline or area of study.

Promote Growth Mindsets

Becoming is better than being.

—Carol Dweck, *Mindset*

Learning depends not just on cognitive ability but also on our beliefs about learning and intelligence, whether we are aware of them or not (Dweck, 2006). One way to scaffold intrinsic motivation is to help children develop growth mindsets. A growth mindset is the belief that one's own skills and abilities can change over time, and that the effort that the learner puts in has a large influence on the outcome. On the other hand, a fixed mindset is a belief that people are endowed with certain skills or levels of intelligence that cannot be changed or transcended.

In a groundbreaking study of beliefs and how they influence motivation and learning, developmental scientists invited kindergartners to enact a series of role-plays using dolls and props. In some cases the child's doll made a mistake (cleaned up a pile of blocks in a way that was too messy or built a house out of LEGO bricks that was missing the windows). They were then given feedback from the teacher that was either person oriented ("The blocks are all crooked and in one big mess. I am very disappointed in you") or process oriented ("The blocks are all crooked and in one big mess. Maybe you could think of *another way* to do it"). Children who were given process-oriented feedback were much more likely to want to try again and felt that continuing to try would be a good option. They generated constructive solutions calling for more effort or new strategies: "I can do it again better if I take my time" or "I'll take it apart and put it together again with windows" (Kamins & Dweck, 1999, p. 840). But when children in the person-oriented feedback group were asked what they wanted to do next, they believed that their setbacks were unchangeable. These children took the critique personally, felt limited by it, and responded accordingly. For example, when asked what the doll that made a mistake should do, typical responses included, "She should cry and go to bed" or "He should get a time out."

Just as we saw in the praise studies above, even positive person-oriented assessments, such as telling children they were smart, promote fixed mindsets. Children who have been told they are intelligent or talented can be paralyzed when they run into a roadblock. Setbacks cause their intrinsic motivation to plummet. These kids may reason, "If I failed, I must not be so smart after all" (Mueller & Dweck, 1998). On the other hand, kids who had heard "You must have tried really hard" before subsequently failing at something kept their intrinsic motivation intact. They tended to believe that ability evolves, that their success resulted from hard work, effort, and practice, that challenges were enjoyable, and that strategies for improvement could readily be generated when needed. A child's mindset can be set up as early as 1 to 3 years old. In one study, toddlers who had had their *efforts* praised (rather than their talents) grew to be 8-year-olds with growth mindsets who were motivated to learn from difficult tasks (Gunderson et al., 2013).

Neuroscience research supports the same pattern. When students with fixed versus growth mindsets took a very difficult exam, the electrical brain signals (ERPs) corresponding with their effort were different. In particular, students with growth mindsets recruited more attentional resources to trying again following error feedback, and they were more likely to correct their mistakes on a surprise retest. Growth mindsets were also associated with brain signals indicating conscious attention to mistakes (Mangels, Butterfield, Lamb, Good, & Dweck, 2006; Moser, Schroder, Heeter, Moran, & Lee, 2011).

Mindsets can affect teachers as well. Garfield High School in Los Angeles was rated one of the worst schools in the city's history. Burnt-out teachers and turned-off students were the norm. But math teacher Jaime Escalante's own growth mindset let him approach the problem as a welcome challenge. Instead of asking, "Can I teach them?" he asked, "How can I teach them?" Instead of "Can they learn?" he wondered, "How will they learn best?" He taught his entire class college-level calculus and brought the students to the national charts in math.

Only three public schools in the country had more students pass the AP Calculus test that year, and both were elite math and science preparatory schools (Dweck, 2006, p. 64). Inner-city Chicago teacher Marva Collins did much the same with her classroom of impoverished 2nd graders. Many of her students had been labeled "retarded" or "emotionally disturbed" and had been kept behind at least one grade. Instead of lowering the bar, Collins applied her own growth mindset to these students and imparted the notion that what any other student could learn, they too could learn, if they were willing to accept the challenge. By the end of the year they had reached 5th grade reading levels, casually discussing Aristotle, Aesop, Tolstoy, Shakespeare, Poe, Frost, and Dickinson (Dweck, 2006).

In one eye-opening study, researchers assessed teachers' mindsets at the beginning of the school year. Those with fixed mindsets about learning—who identified with statements such as, "As a teacher I have no influence on students' intellectual abilities" or "Students' achievement mostly remains constant throughout the year"—finished the year with all of their low-performing students remaining low performing, and all of their high-performing students remaining high performing. But teachers who had growth mindsets, and believed such statements as, "All children can develop their skills" or "I'm not going to let anyone fail," ended the year with both their low-performing and high-performing students earning top performance evaluations (Rheinberg, 2001, cited in Dweck, 2006).

Quick Recap

▶ Students must feel empowered in order to retain their intrinsic motivation.

▶ Teachers must protect curiosity in all classrooms.

▶ Students' beliefs about themselves as learners have a profound impact on their intrinsic motivation and achievement.

▶ Teachers' beliefs and mindsets can affect their students' potential to learn.

Curiosity Technique to Try: Only Assess Effort and Process

In order to shift the culture of learning in your classroom away from externally imposed grades and endpoints, and toward curiosity and intrinsic motivation, try doing a project in which you exclusively assess the effort and process. Alfie Kohn (1999) has recommended that if we must give grades, there should be only two options for students: either "A" or incomplete, because either they have mastered a concept or they are not done learning yet. In this same spirit, we can assess student work based on the quality of effort put in and the process of learning, including how close the students have come to realizing their potential. Suppose that you were doing a 6th grade research project on inventions that have changed society. The students could compile a binder with a step-by-step self-generated plan for completing the project. They could set goals for themselves at each stage of the research process— developing topics, gathering materials, and outlining, paraphrasing, and writing. As their guide, you may meet with them upon the completion of each goal and discuss the process so far. In what way have things been easier or more difficult than they imagined? You can then write up a narrative assessment for them at each stage, noting ideas to expand or narrow their scope, highlighting strengths, and suggesting ways to enhance their effort or process.

Embrace Mistakes

Failure is, in a sense, the highway to success, inasmuch as every discovery of what is false leads us to seek earnestly after what is true.

—John Keats

Making mistakes is an important part of learning. Creativity, change, and innovation are impossible without failure. This is because failing lets us notice the situation from new angles or in finer detail. Something we don't typically hear about is the fact that creative geniuses—people like Albert Einstein or Leonardo da Vinci—have actually had extraordinary failure rates. In fact, there is little evidence that creative geniuses have a higher success rate than any of the rest of us. What often sets them apart is the sheer number of attempts they make. To use a baseball analogy, geniuses simply take more swings at the ball (Sutton, 2009). Not surprisingly, learners with growth mindsets are more likely to expect failure. They view a failure as an opportunity to try again and are more likely to learn from their mistakes (Dweck, 1999).

Failing and expecting failure are important components of letting children take ownership of their education. When my 6-year-old son, Alexei, was learning to ride a bike, we told him that he should plan to have at least 10 bad falls before he found his balance. With this as his expectation, each time he toppled over he felt like he was one step closer to learning to ride. When the episodes of failure are scheduled in, they become like accomplishments unto themselves. Says one math teacher,

> I believe mistakes and failures are all part of the inquiry process. I teach math as the study of patterns, and so when we think we've found a pattern the next step is to test it out. And inevitably we will find lots of things that "don't work," but that's not failure, that's just part of the process. I think in math especially, kids are taught that there is one right answer (and often one right way to find it). I feel that is a dangerous mindset, and it takes me a very long time to get kids comfortable with the idea that math is something that can be played with. Once they have embraced that exploratory mindset, then we can begin to focus on the kinds of mathematical thinking that will help us ask and test better and better questions. "Failures" simply become road signs pointing at better paths.

Students who are not afraid to make mistakes are more likely to take risks in their thinking, question things, allow themselves to be genuinely curious, and remain intrinsically motivated (Kohn, 1999). For the teacher, mistakes offer a window into the process of how a student thinks. If we hold back the urge to correct our students quickly, we can facilitate that learning process. Scaffolding intrinsic motivation requires not just letting students experience failure but also incorporating failure into the path of the learning. Experienced teachers observe closely the mistakes that their students make. They encourage those who have given a good effort, and yet failed.

Stanford University professor Bob Sutton (2009) suggests that when errors happen, we get a window into our deeper learning process. We should ask ourselves, "Am I making errors differently every time? Or do I keep falling into the same traps?" Also, rather than just examining what went wrong, we should be looking at what went right. Ninth grade math teacher Marina Isakowitz is teaching her students to welcome mistakes in her math class. First, she says,

"You have to spend a lot of time and a lot of energy supporting kids to unlearn how they've been taught to learn for the majority of their lives" (wanting to get everything right and please the teacher) (Schwartz, 2014a). Even for her, watching the students struggle involves facing ingrained biases about performance. In order to set up the classroom as a safe space for taking chances and making mistakes, she tells her students, "I'm going to let you bruise yourself, and that's going to be hard to watch, but I'm not going to step in and help" (Schwartz, 2014a). That can feel like she is not doing her job properly, when in fact the opposite is true. Good teachers are guides who can see the big picture because they have a deep understanding of how learning works. Isakowitz has had to hang back and have some faith in what is going to unfold, and that means she too has to unlearn what she previously thought about math education, that students must learn certain skills in a certain order and that they must understand something fully before moving on (Schwartz, 2014a).

The endgame in growing learners, of course, is for them to become robust. To be able to translate what they have learned and to apply the process of coming to discover, ask, and find out to many different situations. Because this is an unpredictable world, becoming robust involves experiencing and learning how to handle failure. This is the opposite of being fragile—or what philosophical essayist Nassim Taleb (2012) has termed "anti-fragile." Those who are anti-fragile go beyond resilience to actually benefit from stress; they love errors because they thrive and grow as a result of volatility. Taleb believes that our overly structured school curriculum and pedagogy have undermined children's ability to develop anti-fragility. The effect of this foible is that what is picked up in the classroom largely stays in the classroom.

Parents and teachers who manipulate and over-control are doing so at the expense of the child's natural love of learning and living. But more than that, by trying to eliminate risk, students are being moved away from their natural state as curious, wondering beings. Instead, says Taleb, we are creating rule-following high achievers who are bound only to the preexisting system that has created them. These standardized learners mindlessly swallow the curriculum. They become like weightlifters who train on fancy machines at the gym but cannot lift a stone out in the world. Learners who can get high grades in precircumscribed subjects but cannot bring themselves to follow their curiosity tend to fall apart when faced with real-life complexity. They become like computers, only slower, in that they are totally untrained to handle ambiguity (Taleb, 2012, p. 244). We should be guiding our children on the path to true intellectual thinking, which emerges out of aimless time and trial and error, from randomness both inside and outside of the classroom. Children need mistakes, mess, adventures, uncertainty, self-discovery, and yes, intrinsic motivation, to learn.

Curiosity Technique to Try: Mark Only Correct Answers

When 3rd grade teacher Paola Velasquez reviews homework, she marks only the questions that the children answered correctly and just leaves incorrect answers clean. When children receive their papers back, they pour over them intently, trying to retrace their thinking and understand their mistakes. Ms. Velasquez's technique has the added bonus of fostering metacognition. These students tend to rework and resubmit the homework with the incorrect questions corrected, even without prompting. Simply shifting the focus from marking what is wrong to marking what is right has completely altered the mindsets of these students.

Encourage Metacognition

Metacognition is the capacity to think about and understand your own thinking. Examples include talking aloud about the thought process while solving a math problem or revealing the steps in making a careful decision (Dichter, 2014). Understanding and knowing one's learning self can be a very powerful tool for branching out in new and interesting ways. Students can learn to step outside their beliefs about themselves and their abilities and come to understand that they are the master in reframing such beliefs—and that they can influence their expectations, feelings, motivation, and behavior.

Metacognition is an important component of the curiosity classroom—if students learn how to control their thinking they become more autonomous and self-regulated learners. In one study, merely asking students to set their own goals improved performance and participation—evidence of autonomy. Specifically, students made and committed to specific goals for their class work near mid-term. The act of identifying ways to improve their performance significantly improved their class participation and performance by virtue of drawing their attention to it (Oppenheimer, 2001).

Curiosity Technique to Try: Reflect in the Third Person

When students are using stories, literature, films, or historical narratives as learning material, you can ask them to keep a journal throughout the term. In their journal, students should record and reflect upon their thoughts about the reading. I like to ask my students to write in their journals about the intersection of the writer's work and their own lives: a time that they felt vulnerable and misunderstood, like Wilbur in *Charlotte's Web*, or discovered something unexpected and shocking like Jane Eyre did. Have they ever seen people act like phonies, like Holden Caulfield did, or tried to impress their peers, like Jay Gatsby did? Have they ever had to take a stand on unethical behavior, like Tom Joad did? What insights have they gained from the way that these characters have handled adversity or opportunity?

Then, at the mid-term, they do a self-assessment of their journal, in which they treat it like a piece of literature itself. They should write a reflection that comments on "the author" (them) and their insights. Does this author seem to be wrestling with particular issues or ideas? What is this journal writer most interested in? Do they seem to be making discoveries of a particular nature? Students should also comment on how the authors of the journal handled the process of writing itself—did they struggle to articulate their thoughts? Take the assignment seriously? Enjoy the process of uncovering new thoughts? As students begin to develop a critical ear and critical voice, it can be very valuable to examine themselves as authors of their own thinking. Indeed, my students report that writing about themselves in the third person, though a bit awkward at first, is a very powerful metacognitive exercise—revealing important understanding of the way they engage and learn.

Relinquish Control

One day, Austin, Texas, high school physics and math teacher Adam Holman finally admitted that his students were not grasping the concepts he was trying to teach them, and realized that he was equally sick of trying to force the information on them. So he changed his teaching style entirely. To begin with, the students had to trust one another and Holman enough to share their weaknesses and vulnerabilities—to articulate their misconceptions of physics and math—and to acknowledge when they were confused. Holman spent lots of time talking about how learning happens and lots of time making sure that the trust was there using ice breakers and trust games. He asked his students to show him that they had learned the material, no matter how long it took them, and they would do well in the course (Schwartz, 2014b).

Switching grading policies and assigning hands-on lessons all helped Holman's students feel he trusted and respected them. And they rose to the challenge: "I think the kids were just waiting to be let loose and to be treated like adults" (Schwartz, 2014b).

Research studies confirm that giving control to students leads to better learning. In one 2nd grade classroom, when the teacher threw out the math textbook and reward system and allowed students to move around the classroom and take on work from their own initiative, form groups, and figure out their own solutions to problems, they added sophisticated reasoning skills to the basic understanding of concepts (Yackel, Cobb, & Wood, 1991). In a high school chemistry class, when students did their labs without clear-cut instructions, deciding for themselves the strategies to try for solving problems, they reproduced better lab reports and understood the material more deeply than those students who were told exactly what to do. The students felt a great sense of pride in the fact that they carried out the experiments on their own (Rainey, 1965).

Letting go of control requires taking a leap of faith. Some teachers worry that more progressive approaches will suck up time and leave them in a situation where they can't possibly cover everything in the jam-packed curriculum (Schwartz, 2014b). Other teachers claim that they would love to let the students choose or run the curriculum, but that that decision is not theirs to make. Even without the discretion to let the students choose the topics or the methods of study, teachers can relinquish some of their control and give it to the students by letting the students frame the lesson. For example, in a high school English class, assemble a list of novels and brief descriptions that would satisfy the standards. Let the students vote on which ones they will read as a class. Or better yet, let each student select the three novels that he or she will focus on for the term. You can assemble study groups made up of the students who chose coming of age novels or those who chose science fiction. They can meet and discuss throughout the semester or even be assessed together.

If the curriculum is more tightly prescribed, you might also ask your students to reflect on *why* the subject matter was chosen for them to study. What about it did some person or group think was so important? Let the students decide which specific parts of the general topic to delve into. Begin all units by asking students to talk about what they already know about the subject and what they would like to know (Kohn, 1993).

Curiosity Technique to Try: Open Prompt Essays

Augustana College professor Laura Greene writes that her intellectual life began when, as a junior in college, instead of being given a prompt, she was forced to write a paper about *Jane Eyre* that answered her own question. Up until that point, she had been highly successful in school due to her being unusually perceptive about gleaning and producing exactly what her teachers wanted. But once there was no hidden answer to guess at in her writing, Greene suddenly became interested in answering a question that would satisfy herself. For the first time in her education, she had a stake in her own learning. After that, the world was different (Greene, 2005).

To make children into thinkers or writers, teachers need to develop in them a strong interest in real things that are going on in the world around them. The best thing is for students to write about what they are very interested in. And yet, teachers most often do exactly the reverse, assign restrictive writing prompts, and thus kill the spontaneous beauty, individuality, and vitality of the child's voice (Vygotsky, 1967/2004). There is nothing more harmful to the child's thinking than giving her a topic about which she has thought little and on which she has nothing much to say. My first-year college students are also always horrified when the first essay rolls around and the topic is open. That is, until they realize that they are suddenly free to write about something genuine that they themselves care about. This takes a shift in their mentality about the point of writing, and indeed, the point of school. But if we guide our students in developing their own questions and topics—if we give them a chance to rediscover what they are interested in—their intrinsic drive to learn will be awakened, and there will be no looking back.

In Sum

Children are endlessly curious and motivated to learn when they enter school, but this intrinsic motivation is in danger of becoming squashed by constant surveillance and judgments in the form of due dates, grades, and testing. Even praise can influence curiosity negatively, since praise causes the learner to look outward and, at times, to become overly self-conscious.

On the other hand, when learners are given the power and respect to guide their own interests to fruition, when they come up with their own ideas to solve problems, and when they are allowed to make mistakes and learn from them, their intrinsic motivation significantly increases. Likewise, if we want to keep our students curious, we need to promote growth mindsets—beliefs that challenges are enjoyable, that abilities grow and evolve over time, and that effort and practice and the process of learning are more important than the outcomes. Teachers with growth mindsets themselves, who allow their students freedom to explore solutions to problems, develop higher-performing students who are more robust in the face of setbacks.

Bolster Imagination
and Creativity

Alice laughed. "There's no use trying," she said,
"one can't believe impossible things." "I daresay
you haven't had much practice," said the Queen. . . .
"Why, sometimes I've believed as many as six
impossible things before breakfast."

—Lewis Carroll, *Alice's Adventures in Wonderland*

Our imaginations let us envision possibilities. They allow us to try on and form new ideas, which may or may not be directly experienced by our senses. Imagination is the basis of all our creative action—anything we make or alter or envision or combine—and therefore, it is at the root of all intellectual life, from art to science to technological innovation. As eminent developmental psychologist Lev Vygotsky once said, "Absolutely everything around us that was created by the hand of man, the entire world of human culture, as distinct from the world of nature, all this is the product of human imagination and of creation based on this imagination" (1967/2004, pp. 9–10).

Children's lives are filled with narratives (films, games, television shows, and storybooks) that feature the fantastical and impossible. For instance, children's books overwhelmingly star animals that talk, wear clothes, drive cars, and have human dilemmas. We would be hard pressed to find a popular children's series that did not feature furry or feathered friends. This is so much the case that little children have been known to approach wild animals, expecting a greeting or an invitation for tea! Depending on their belief system, adults respond to imaginative children in a variety of ways. Hindu parents may believe that a child's invisible friend is a manifestation of the spiritual plane and an entrée into the child's past life. They see participation in imaginary worlds as a serious activity and tend to encourage it well into childhood. On the other hand, Mennonite families regard pretending as a waste of time stemming from the idleness that can harm children's development. As a result, Mennonite parents typically discourage children from reading books that contain fantasy, magic, and myths. Likewise, fundamentalist Christian parents have expressed negative attitudes about imaginary friends or invented characters like fairies and witches, sometimes equating such imagining with deceit or the devil (Taylor & Carlson, 2000). Regardless of how the child's pastimes are perceived, one thing is certain, everywhere that there are children, there will be play and imagination, pretend and creativity (Goncu, Jain, & Tuermer, 2007). These are reliable manifestations of children's inherent curiosity.

The story *Harold and the Purple Crayon* by Crockett Johnson is the epitome of the child's journey of imagination. It begins when Harold, after thinking it over for some time, decides to take a walk in the moonlight. He uses his purple crayon to draw the moon and the path, and when the straight line is a bit too straight, Harold draws himself right off the path and through a shortcut across the field. The shortcut leads him to a place where he thinks a forest ought to be, but not wanting to get lost, he draws a very small forest filled with apple trees. In a while, when Harold imagines and creates a sandy beach, that reminds him of picnics and he begins to get hungry. So he draws a simple picnic lunch—nothing but pie. But thankfully, Harold draws all nine kinds of pie that he likes best! Harold, like all children, uses his imagination to create, experience, and learn within a world of his own invention.

The Development of Imagination

Toddlers engage in imaginary and pretend play as early as 18 months. As child development expert Jean Piaget (1973) described, imagination emerges out of imitation. First, babies use their reflexes as they experience the ambient world—leaning toward the light, looking at faces, paying attention to sounds and gestures. Then, their behavior becomes more deliberate—they begin imitating sounds, mimicking a parent's facial expression, and turn taking in little pretend conversations. Imitating, with the help of curiosity and motivation, develops into more complex symbolic play and invention. Toddlers begin to pretend a banana is a phone or feed a doll using a stick for a spoon (Singer & Singer, 2013).

Children's imagination helps them make sense of the world as it is, and at the same time, crack open that place among their accumulated experiences, established pathways, and the enormity of possibility to transcend reality as known (Greene, 1995). Between the ages of 2 and 3, children might imagine that a box is a house, computer, dog crate, and so on. They sometimes use toys to reproduce known actions and variations (like driving in a sofa car or walking stuffed dogs). One time, my 3-year-old nephew, Leo, was visiting and wanted to call his dad. He picked up the phone and began a quiet conversation, no real words, but all the actions involved in the phone calls he sees every day—dialing, holding the phone to his ear, the rising and falling tone of voice and pauses. He mimicked his mom, down to the detail of whispering to keep his pretend conversation private.

Gradually, kids increase the complexity of pretend play with step-by-step planning. When guided by speech, this leads to the creation of invented narratives in which events are threaded on to each other (Diachenko, 2011). By 4 to 5 years old, the imagining child may be filling a bucket with mud and pretending that it's a birthday cake then putting stick candles on it. She knows that this is mud she's playing with, not a real cake, but it easily becomes a suitable cake for an imaginary friend's birthday party.

What is interesting about make-believe play is that the child can understand the rules of reality and can also choose to leave reality behind. Disengaging from the real and moving into the fantastical is a choice, but a choice with limits. The rules of the culture and laws of physics tend to be preserved even in the face of the pretend. For example, Harold does not draw a forest floating in the water or a skyscraper covered with doors. Children will not pretend to chew imaginary juice from a play cup or make-believe that they are sleeping standing up. Kids maintain the presence of mind to discern the difference between pretend and real. If they are imagining that there are pencils in a case, a child will not send someone looking for a real pencil to the empty case (Woolley & Phelps, 1994). In one study, kindergartners refused to engage in dramatic play with cubes that had faces painted on them. The children said that cubes could only be used to build things; they could not be used as babies in their game of "house" (Gasparova, 1985, cited in Diachenko, 2011). My daughter Sonia treats her most beloved doll, Baby Goo-Goo, as a member of the family in every way. She talks to her and speaks Goo-Goo's falsetto voice in response. She feeds and dresses and sleeps with her. She asks us to babysit when she heads off to her pretend work. But when I mention that Goo-Goo might be tired or excited, Sonia is quick to remind me, "Mommy, she's not real." Imagination is the one means by which a child's knowledge can be widened without direct experience. Children use fantasy to break down the world into units they can explore and manipulate, eventually incorporating that understanding into their schemas of life (Diachenko, 2011).

Imagination Supports Curiosity

Imaginative role-playing is a sophisticated cognitive skill. It involves planning with other actors in real time, creating role-appropriate voices and actions, and imagining the thoughts and feelings of the character one is playing (Brill, 2004). Imaginative children show superior cognitive development and academic success. For one thing, fantasy play encourages private speech, which is a boon for learning. While pretending, children talk out loud to themselves to plan and direct their own actions, identify their feelings, and guide their attention. With time, that inner voice becomes internalized and turns into thoughts (Luria, 1961). Children who use private speech excel in problem solving. In one study, 3-year-olds were asked to press a button when a red light came on, and to not press it when a blue light came on. This inhibition task was very difficult for the children. They were unable to stop the urge to press, regardless of the color of the light they saw. Next, they were told to say to themselves "press" or "don't press" when the light came on. Their performance skyrocketed (Luria, 1961). While playing in imaginary scenarios, children spend lots of time in private speech—talking themselves through the decisions and procedures that they need as they go.

Imaginative play also develops the child's vocabulary. While playing, kids get a chance to try out many, many words. They practice with future tense most often, saying things like, "First we'll do this" or "How about this?" Or, when planning a mud-pie birthday party, "First we'll make the cake, then we'll sing." "How about I work at the bakery?" "No, how about you are cooking the cake at home and someone else brings another cake from the bakery?" These are complex communicative maneuvers—planning with other actors and engaging in role-play, including voicing the imaginary characters (Singer & Singer, 2013). In one research study, scientists discovered that 4-year-olds who engaged in lots of dramatic play developed more advanced vocabularies as compared with those who did not. Their speech also contained more complex sentence structure (Levy, Wolfgang, & Koorland, 1992).

In addition to expanding the child's vocabulary, pretend play provides great practice in being flexible. If a child doesn't have the object she needs for the game, she can make something else stand in for that object, just like when Harold needed a boat to traverse the water. He drew one just in the nick of time (Johnson, 2005; Singer & Singer, 2013). Children who use their imaginations more and engage in more fantasy play in 1st and 2nd grades score higher on measures of divergent thinking in the 11th and 12th grades (Russ, 2003). Divergent thinking has been named as the number one desirable skill for 21st century success (Pappano, 2014).

Children can learn new information (like names for never before encountered objects or things those objects can do) in a pretend game and then apply that knowledge to their next situation (Hopkins, Dore, & Lillard, 2015). In imaginative play, children also can consider what the world would be like if alternative events had happened. For example, by role-playing, 4-year-old Sonia can envision our family dynamics if she had been born first and was now the big sister to Alexei. (It is an exciting prospect to her, since she always loses races and has to defer to her elder brother's ideas!) Research shows that imagination allows children to predict and plan for consequences by creating models of the world and then comparing reality to those models. "What if we moved to Mars?" or "What if we lived in a tree house?" are scenarios that can be imagined as a simulation for solving problems or predicting behavior (Weisberg & Gopnik, 2013). Using imagination, children can understand ideas from another person's point of view. As an example, when students role-play stories, they can comprehend greater complexities in the narrative and remember the content more precisely (Marbach & Yawkey, 1980). In other words, fantasy play allows the child to integrate that new sense of reality into his everyday experience (Bouldin, 2006).

Socioemotional Effects of Imagination

From a very young age, children who participate in more fantasy, make-believe, and imaginative activities can better regulate their emotions and feel empathy (Smith & Mathur, 2009). In one study, preschoolers whose imaginative pretend play included impersonating others (playing the father or the teacher, for instance) were better at understanding others' emotions than children who did not impersonate (Taylor, Carlson, Maring, Gerow, & Charley, 2004). Kids who are great pretenders are more skilled at inferring and predicting the thoughts and feelings of others (Schwebel, Rosen, & Singer, 1999).

In a classic *Calvin and Hobbes* cartoon strip, we get to see Calvin's day at school the way he experiences it. First, he is moved through a cattle pen, then he is put on a conveyer belt, his head sawed off and filled with a green liquid like the other bottles going by. Next Calvin gasps for breath on a hamster wheel, hammers railroad ties in jailbird striped garb, walks around repeating things as a robot and a parrot, gets hammered into a cube shape to fit in a cube-sized hole, and gasps for air as a fish out of water. Finally, when the school day is out, Calvin is able to escape into his imagination—he copes with school's burdens by flying down the hill with Hobbes, his philosophical stuffed tiger (Watterson, 2013).

When difficult situations arise, children often use make-believe as a needed getaway. Children with more developed imaginations use more effective methods to deal with their problems (Goldstein & Russ, 2000). When children use make-believe to understand feelings of insecurity, they suddenly gain control over them. In one experiment, researchers observed 3-year-olds on their very first day of preschool. The children who showed the highest levels of anxiety were given the option to either listen to a story or engage in dramatic free play. Those children who chose free play reduced their anxiety much more effectively than the group who listened to a story. Their play was also strikingly imaginative, indicating that they had used the creative outlet as a conflict resolution mechanism (Barnett, 1984).

One of more adaptive aspects of make-believe play is self-control. When children play together, if one of them becomes disruptive, the other children will not want to play with her any longer. So children learn that in order to play, you have to be cooperative and helpful and you have to share. This is an important function of play for social behavior. Via imaginative play, kids quickly learn that they cannot cheat, they have to be fair, and they have to carefully consider their neighbor. Children who undermine the rules are eliminated. Very imaginative children tend to be more cooperative. They share better and help each other more. They begin to develop a sense of self and a sense of morality (Singer & Singer, 2013).

Lauded writers, scientists, inventors, and contributors to society, including the writers Johann Wolfgang von Goethe, Leo Tolstoy, and the Bronte sisters, all imagined and played incessantly when they were children (Root-Bernstein & Root-Bernstein, 1999). Grown-ups, too, benefit from imaginative thoughts and

---

Quick Recap

▶ Imagination is at the root of all creativity and innovation.

▶ Participating in imaginary worlds is a serious act for developing children.

▶ Imagination can widen students' knowledge without the need for direct experience.

▶ Imaginative children thrive in many cognitive domains, including private speech, vocabulary, planning, perspective-taking, and flexibility.

▶ Imaginative children are superior in emotional regulation, coping, and impulse control.

fantasies. In a classic study, adults who reported rich fantasy lives better controlled compulsive behaviors over those who reported being unimaginative. Specifically, those people with a dynamic imagination were able to write extremely slowly, or sit quietly in a room without restlessness while waiting in an interview. They were able to restrain impulsive actions and thoughts much more readily (McCraven, Singer, & Wilensky, 1956). Never underestimate the importance of imagination in children—it paves the road to an effective, satisfying, and creative adulthood. "To the extent that the main educational objective of teaching is guidance of school children's behavior so as to prepare them for the future, development, and exercise of the imagination should be one of the main forces enlisted for the attainment of this goal" (Vygotsky 1967/2004, p. 88). In other words, imagination belongs at the forefront of the curiosity classroom.

Envision

Using imagination to envision a learning experience can improve performance in and of itself. When you vividly imagine the details of yourself delivering that killer speech, to your mind and brain the act of imagining may be the same as practicing the speech itself. Research shows that when we zone in on the image of our bodies doing specific actions, we increase the likelihood of actual success. Our human brains have evolved to learn quickly and efficiently, by both actively experiencing things and also by "almost" experiencing, meaning that we do not have to directly do something ourselves to get it. Part of being highly social creatures is the adaptation to learn from others and from our surrounds. Coaches have had great success in guiding competitive athletes in imagery of such domains as shooting free throws in basketball (Post, Wrisberg, & Mullins, 2010), mastering gymnastics routines (Post & Wrisberg, 2012), and hitting difficult golf shots (Smith, Wright, & Cantwell, 2008), to name a few examples. New research shows us that the brain can even train muscles and increase strength just by envisioning a movement. In one elegant experiment, students who merely imagined themselves working out the muscles of one arm significantly increased their strength in the relevant muscle groups. When electrical potentials in the parts of the brain associated with muscle strength were measured, they showed that their mental training was no different from physical training (Ranganathan, Siemionow, Liu, Sahgal, & Yue, 2004).

In another stunning study, two groups of people without piano playing experience were taught a brief lesson on a one-handed, five-finger piano melody. The first group practiced the melody on the piano for two hours a day for five days. The second group merely imagined that they were doing the exercise, visualizing as precisely as possible that they were practicing on the piano. The brains of those who played and imagined playing *both* showed structural changes in the area of the brain related to the movement of the fingers. Equally astonishing, the group that had only imagined playing significantly improved in their ability to play the piano melody (Pascual-Leone et al., 1995). These studies show us the great power that imagination holds for learning. Imagination should be harnessed in students and funneled into the classroom work they are doing.

Curiosity Technique to Try: Imagine a World

With their imaginations, students can enter make-believe worlds to understand complex topics. One method is called the IEPC Strategy, which stands for Imagine, Elaborate, Predict, and Confirm. This technique capitalizes on the fact that students learn new materials more readily when images are vividly attached to them (Tindall-Ford & Sweller, 2006). One middle school teacher discovered that the examples he gave on food webs and ecosystems were not quite gelling for his students. It was not until he asked them to create their own imaginary ecosystems, with made-up plants, animals, and environmental niches, that they were really able to understand the concepts. Once they mastered the relationships within their make-believe world, they could easily make the leap to the real world ecosystem design (Smith & Mathur, 2009). My colleague, psychologist and anthropologist Richard Zimmer, used the same strategy in his college-level seminar. To scaffold students' learning about the structures required for a civic and just society to function, he arranged for groups of students to spend the semester imagining and creating a new human settlement on Mars, which they could invent from the ground up. Each year the students would build upon the imaginary society that the previous group had envisioned. The experience left the students with a hands-on, make-believe model to draw upon when trying to understand the complexities of city planning, educational design, civic engagement, law, and public service and responsibility.

There are many new simulation gaming platforms that can be used to model and experience real world situations for better understanding. To illustrate, in *Evolution: The Game of Intelligent Life*, players guide and control animals' adaptation to their environments and evolution; in *3rd World Farmer*, players make decisions on how to thrive despite corruption, scant resources, and political and natural disasters; in *Wolf Quest*, students can learn what it is like to live in Yellowstone National Park as a wolf; and in *ElectroCity*, students build and manage their own towns in terms of energy and environmental impacts. Supreme Court justice Sandra Day O'Connor has developed a series of games called *Supreme Decision*, in which players must investigate and argue real court cases.

Tell Stories

The stars we are given. The constellations we make. That is to say, stars exist in the cosmos, but constellations are the imaginary lines we draw between them, the readings we give the sky, the stories we tell.

—Rebecca Solnit, *Storming the Gates of Paradise*

Storytelling is an ancient and intimate tradition, dating back to the earliest beginnings of human language. In a classroom, storytelling can be an active exercise of the imagination, which contributes to the curiosity classroom and enhances learning. The story cannot teach students by itself—the reader of the story has to collaborate. The job of the teacher is to set up that collaboration, guide you to the stories that will have meaning for you, and provoke you to engage with them (Finkel, 2000).

An important component to scaffolding students' interests is helping students find some personal or intimate reflection of themselves in the lesson. That is true of our experience with the novel, the film, or the painting—art and intellectual pursuits are only effective to the extent that people can identify with them. The hero of the novel is meant to represent us in some small way. We are meant to feel their pain and triumph and to be relieved that the artist found a way to bring those complicated, almost indescribable, subtle human emotions to the concrete. We can finally experience and explain those particular feelings. Incidentally, neuroscientist and middle school teacher Judy Willis has shown that in order to motivate students, we must tap into the dopamine systems of their brains—which are activated first and foremost by self-interest. Willis (2012) has discovered that to get middle school students interested in math, it must be about them. Thus the expression "research is me-search" among scientists. We are endlessly interested in our unique, but shared, experience. Again, the basis for all motivation is the survival of the self. Where are our students and what are they interested in? We can only know by letting them drive the knowing; by beginning with who they are.

Canadian neuroscientist Raymond Mar and his colleagues at York University study the effects of storytelling on the brain. They recently compared the findings of nearly one hundred experiments of human social relationships. These scientists pinpointed that the brain networks activated when we understand others' beliefs overlap significantly with those neural networks we use when we read or hear stories. In a sense, when we read or hear stories, our brain treats them as simulations of our real lived social experiences (Mar, 2011). In a related study, Mar and his colleagues found that the more stories preschoolers had had read to them, the more skilled they were at understanding the perspectives of others (Mar, Tackett, & Moore, 2010). Reading to children, telling stories, and encouraging pretend play all influence children's social understanding and skills. We need to empower children to tell their stories, not only so we can hear them, but also so they can allow their own rationality and social skills to emerge (Greene, 1995; Leslie, 2014).

Curiosity Technique to Try: Collaborative Stories

Young students can participate in stories by repeating phrases or responding to characters. When the pigeon in Mo Willems's children's classic asks, "Hey, can I drive the bus?" students can shout out their responses. When students add hand gestures or sound effects, like snapping for the rain, they immerse themselves in the imaginary narrative. Story weaving is another method of using imagination and narrative to garner curiosity. When story weaving, one person (sometimes the teacher) begins the story, but passes the baton along, and the children invent it as they go. As mentioned above, this can even be done in chat rooms, using software like DailyMeet. We do this in my classes with poetry. It can be even more exciting to see where the narratives go when the next person in line only receives a part of the poem or story in progress. We fold the paper over to hide everything but the most recent line. Reenacting myths or popular stories is also an effective way of comprehending complex lessons (Smith & Mathur, 2009).

Allow students to become emotionally tied to the stories you read by inventing role-plays. When playing a role, students get to live the part and become the character, but they also get to collaborate and understand each actor's role in a narrative as a complex series of interactions. Instead of just writing a report on the U.S. justice system, assign children roles (e.g., judge, jury member, court bailiff) and have them research the role and present cogent, reasonable responses as they enact a real courtroom scene (Siegelman, 2003).

Curiosity Technique to Try: Math Stories

Education philosopher and writer Kieran Egan (1989) believes that all domains of knowledge can be taught using forms of storytelling. The more abstract and removed a topic is from a student's daily intentions and emotions, the more that subject matter needs to be put in a narrative form in order to be understood. There are several narratives that provide an entry point and larger context of math. Books such as *The Number Devil* can be used as a jumping-off point for exploring the history of numbers and number theory, *The Beauty of Numbers* can focus students on number patterns in art and nature, or *Time and Place* can connect celestial navigation to a way to study geometry.

For a math lesson on integers, number sense, and counting, Egan proposes that the teacher's first job is to convey to the students how wonderful—almost magical—the decimal system really is. When we expose the ingenuity of mathematics, things that we take so casually, like counting, become linked to the amazing achievements that produced them. To display the difference between number sense and counting, Egan suggests beginning with the scientific findings that show that many animals have number sense, but only humans can count. For example, there is a species of wasp, genus *Eumenes*, whose females are much larger than the males. The mother wasp knows which grubs will grow into males and which will grow into females, and she doubles the amount of food for the female grubs. At this point in the lesson, telling the story of the farmer's grain can cement the distinction between inherent number sense and more complex, learned counting.

> [There was a crow] eating the farmer's grain. The farmer had decided to shoot the crow. It had made its nest in the barn. But whenever the farmer approached the barn the crow flew away. When he left the barn, the crow flew back. Thinking to trick the crow, the farmer took a friend with him to the barn. The farmer stayed in the barn while the friend left. But the crow was not fooled, and stayed in his tree until the farmer came out too. The next day the farmer took two friends with him to the barn, and he stayed behind when the two friends left. But still the crow waited till he came out before returning to its nest. The next day the farmer took three friends, with the same result. Next he took four, and then five friends. When the five came out, the farmer remaining behind, the crow flew back to its nest, and the farmer shot it. (Egan, 1989, p. 79)

The crow's number sense is about the same as ours is—once numbers reach about five or six, it can no longer precisely distinguish them. This can be displayed viscerally by asking students to guess the number of marbles in your hand when you quickly open and close them. They will have no trouble with small numbers, but as the number of marbles exceeds five or six, they will have to report to the more complex skill of counting. You can then go into the methods that humans have developed to count, a fascinating story in itself.

Create

Creativity is wanting to know, digging deeper, looking twice, listening for smells, talking listening to a cat, crossing out mistakes, getting in, getting out, having a ball, cutting holes to see through, cutting corners, plugging into the sun, building sand castles, singing in your own key, shaking hands with tomorrow.

—Ellis Paul Torrance, "The Nature of Creativity as Manifest in Its Testing," in *The Nature of Creativity*

Creativity is imagination in action. It is the tangible of insights and ideas, art and design. According to Frank Barron, pioneer of the psychology of creativity, the ingredients of creativity are recognizing patterns, making connections, taking risks, challenging assumptions, taking advantage of chance, and seeing in new ways (1988, p. 78). Creativity involves both divergent thinking (often in the form of brainstorming ideas in a setting free from restrictions and fear of criticism) and convergent thinking (integrating facts, summarizing, and inter-preting), in order for decision making and action to take place (Smith & Mathur, 2009). Highly creative people are good at marshaling both types of thinking and at knowing when to alternate among them (Bronson & Merryman, 2010).

Creative and innovative people mix and remix ideas. They spot patterns and break through them, finding new ways to see things (Leslie, 2014). For instance, successful artists and innovators are often experts in the knowl-edge of their domains before branching out and breaking the molds of those disciplines. Even artists like Pablo Picasso, who reimagined how to represent people and objects in the world with his wild and surreal shapes and colors, first mastered the techniques of classical painting at Spain's foremost tradi-tional art school. If we trace the history of great works and discoveries, they are most often the result of an enormous amount of previously accumulated experience (Vygotsky, 1967/2004).

The best thing we can do to support learning in children (or adults, for that matter) is to provide as many diverse, visceral experiences as possible. When it comes to formal education, then, building a strong foundation for creativity in students involves broadening the types of experiences we provide them with. The more children see, hear, and experience, the more they will expand their senses of possibility. The more elements of reality they have in their repertoire, the more productive their imaginations can be (Vygotsky, 1967/2004). The more energetic and lively children's imaginations, the more facts in their minds will find themselves in new combinations. Frameworks can take on new meaning or new emotional coloring. Physics, math, and history, for example, are not disciplines to be learned separately from imaginative growth. The imagination has to grow in these disciplines, so that the child's grasp on the world is enriched with meaning (Egan, 1997).

Recently I took my 4- and 6-year-old kids to the Maker Faire, an exhibition and interactive celebration of a grassroots, technology-infused community of do-it-yourself-ers. It is the zenith of imagination. There, hobbyists from personal garages and shared innovation places (called hacker-spaces), high school students, and engineering firms alike showed what they had invented and invited us to make stuff along with them. Makers have created a warm, open-sourced culture—one of sharing blueprints, knowledge, and tools; talking about ideas; exploring possibilities, and trying things out. Creating there is informal and peer-led, it is done for no other purpose than fun and the self-fulfillment of doing it. My kids and I spent our day in the underwater world of a neon-glowing inflated nylon coral reef within a darkened warehouse, watching giant smoke-ring-breathing dragons ride by; powering an electric guitar band by pedaling bicycles; observing robots the size of a marbles making Zen-inspired mandalas in white sand trays; and launching paper rockets to the ceiling using bike pumps. Many of the most creative experiences we had were spontaneous—like joining other parents and children in the making of a dome of straws. It could not have been planned because it simply bubbled up out of the shared minds of the group.

When it comes to inspiring creativity, virtual experiences are never as powerful as lived ones (Singer & Singer, 2013). It is much more valuable and inspiring for creativity to go to the circus and see the animals perform than to watch them do tricks on TV. At the circus, you hear the noises, you smell the smells, you see the responses of others, you observe the ambient culture, you feel the excitement of the crowd, you know that the tight-rope walker does not have strings attached to her, and you see the animals actually being fed. Television, movies, and video games do not encourage imagination as much as visceral experiences because their stories are largely predetermined. When children spend too much time in front of a screen, they play and use their imaginations less. They have diminished practice with creating the narratives, so they create less complex ones. When kids play following screen time, they may imitate a story they have seen. That actually usurps their ability to create something unique. In an important research study, viewing television and video stories significantly stifled the ability of 10- to 12-year-old children to tell and write their own imaginative stories (Belton, 2001). Good teachers help to direct the curiosity of children, by offering authentic experiences, building their store of knowledge, and making creativity a daily possibility.

Curiosity Technique to Try:
Create Something with Found Objects

Go on a walk and collect objects. Depending on your focus, you may want to look for items in nature or do a cleanup and find treasures within the trash. You can contact local manufacturing companies and ask for remnants, or visit the town recycle center swap shop. Have your students conduct some preliminary research on what they would like to build. Maybe they want to make machines or perhaps sculptures. If you limit the materials to found objects, you will be surprised what will be possible. For inspiration, send your students to websites that feature art installations and projects made with grassroots found objects, like www.makerfaire.com and www.burningman.org.

Create a box city! In 1969, art teacher Ginny Graves and her architect husband Dean Graves came up with the first lesson plan for Box City, an innovative and interdisciplinary program that uses ordinary cardboard boxes (of any size and shape; upcycled and repurposed from the real community) to give students hands-on experience with community planning and architectural design. The students make their own buildings from cardboard boxes and then combine the boxes into a functioning community using a base plan and taking into account geography, economics, ecology, history, and multiple cultures. Throughout every step of the process, the students come to understand the built environments that we live in. In a box city, communities are created organically and the way that real communities develop—with a mix of regulation, collaboration, necessity, and entrepreneurship. Students may hold mock town meetings, playing roles of developers, government officials, neighborhood representatives, and environmental activists—all of the people with a stake in city planning decisions. One main goal of Box City is to help people to feel empowered to participate in civic processes, rather than remaining helpless (www.cubekc.org). Making a Box City helps students take responsibility for their actions, think of others and themselves, and work with boxes—materials that are often just broken down and discarded.

Let Go

Children will create . . . Whether order or disorder, chaos or harmony, beauty or ugliness, accord or violence, they will create.

—David Orr, Foreword in *The Third Teacher*

It takes both faith and time to activate creativity. Letting go of schedules and structure can allow the imagination to open up. Daydreaming is an important part of realizing creative goals, because it helps us to move back and forth between focused attention and inattention (Zhong, 2012). Similarly, in order to be creative, we must be willing to indulge distractions. The best ideas often come from letting the mind go wherever it wants. Research shows that when the brain is between thoughts or tasks, it is actually quite active. It is no surprise that people who daydream consistently score higher on measures of creativity (Singer & McCraven, 1961). This is why writers and artists carry around sketchpads and notebooks—they can jot down little things that happen or surprise them—things they read about or observe. Composers scramble to write down melodies that arrive in their heads, even as they wake from dreaming them. Schubert wrote on bar napkins. Investing time and energy into slowing down and noticing as a way of life is just the beginning (Kaufman, 2013).

When our minds are relaxed, our brains go into a state of quiet, restful peace. They move away from the vigilant and critical thinking of the cerebral cortex and begin to produce a type of electrical signal called alpha waves. Neuroscientists have shown that in this state, our attention systems focus inward and that we can listen to the quiet ideas inside of our heads. When our brains are producing alpha waves, we tend to have insights (Kounios & Beeman, 2009). That explains why we experience so many good ideas when walking quietly in the woods, jogging to music, or taking warm showers. Even sleeping can help people perform better at finding creative solutions to difficult problems (McNerney, 2012).

Patty Kean, who works with adolescent students with learning disabilities, began a Not-a-Writer Writing Group in order to encourage creativity without judgment in her students. She and three students agreed to meet during a free period to meditate for seven minutes, write for seven minutes, read what they wrote (with passing as an option, but one that was never used), and respond with what they noticed and what touched them. Each student and the teacher then asked one question each. All in the group (including Kean) had been told and believed that they were handicapped in writing. But in this relaxed and nurturing space week after week, "just writing" and being present encouraged them to write profound poetry, narratives, essays, and storybook rhymes. The group members opted to continue meeting, and even asked if they could meet during the summer using Skype.

When we fill every idle second of our lives or our children's lives, we show our lack of faith in human creativity. Learning in school, which depends on intrinsic motivation, also depends on nourishing the seeds that germinate during times of boredom or impatience. One of the greatest gifts we can give children as they become lifelong learners is to teach them to relax. That means bringing themselves into focus and establishing a way to drop down into more alpha wave thinking. Indeed, moving quickly from task to task does not allow the brain to ever get into the deeper state, where interesting and creative things can emerge.

Curiosity Technique to Try: Assign Doodling

Many of us doodle when we listen, whether consciously or unconsciously. Doodling is relaxing, but it also guides our attention and concentration; it keeps us at optimal arousal levels and allows us to remain focused on the task at hand. In a recent study, people were asked to listen to a long, rambling voicemail message in which a woman mentioned who would be attending an upcoming party. One group was instructed to sit still and just listen. A second group was asked to doodle as they listened. The doodling group was significantly better at naming the attendees of the party immediately afterwards, and they did 30 percent better on a surprise memory test of the names (Andrade, 2010). Try assigning students to doodle during class. You can create a doodle notebook or assign them to doodle during times of listening. Ask students to reflect upon their attention while doodling or do a doodle content analysis. You can assign an incidental art project in which they expand upon one of their doodles and enhance it. Doodles can even be combined to create a class mural.

Improvise

When in doubt, make a fool of yourself. There is a microscopically thin line between being brilliantly creative and acting like the most gigantic idiot on earth. So what the hell, leap.

—Cynthia Heimel

In order to emerge, creativity must be spontaneous. In one recent study, researchers looked at the brains of jazz musicians during periods of improvisation. What they discovered was that the part of the brain associated with self-expression and storytelling (called the medial prefrontal cortex) was also activated during improvisation. It was as if these musicians were telling stories with their music! Equally as compelling was their discovery that the part of the brain that plans and controls impulses and holds us back from making fools of ourselves (the dorsolateral prefrontal cortex) was *deactivated* during improvisation. On the other hand, when the musicians in the study were asked

Quick Recap

- To the mind and brain, vividly imagining is no different than doing.
- Storytelling is an ancient, highly effective teaching and meaning-making technique.
- Through stories, students can come to identify with and understand complexity.
- Stories help with motivation, perspective-taking, and comprehension.
- Creativity springs out of experiencing, taking risks, and seeing things in new ways.
- Lived experiences are important for learning.
- Unstructuring, letting go, and relaxing allow creative ideas to emerge.

to play a piece in exact form, from rote memory, the impulse control centers of their brains activated once again (Limb & Braun, 2008).

There is an element of improvisation in any creative act—of being open to whatever may happen. Likewise, there is the same openness in being an engaged learner. The entire endeavor of high-quality teaching, one could argue, is much more akin to improvisation than it is to learning scripts. The most powerful way to develop creativity in your students is to be a role model. Children develop creativity not when you tell them to, but when you show them. The teachers you most remember from your school days are not those who crammed the most content into their lectures, but those who were willing to take their own intellectual risks, be spontaneous, and go with surprising turns of events that come up so often in the classroom. The teachers you remember are those whose thoughts and actions served as your role models. Most likely they balanced teaching content with teaching you how to think with and about that content, how to transform that content using your own imagination (Sternberg & Williams, 1996).

Curiosity Technique to Try: Show Me How

A fun way to get students to loosen up and open to the creativity of improvisation is to look at things in their world in new ways. This can be done with an improvisation game called Show Me How. Young children can respond with their bodies to "Show me how" directives (e.g., "Show me how you tie your shoe"; Show me how you greet a new friend"). As children move into the primary grades they can incorporate elements that include the experience of different emotions (e.g., "Show me how it feels to taste something sweet"). Then, older children can be challenged with more complex social and emotional responses (e.g., "Show me how it feels to be left out"; "Show me how it feels to fall in love"; "Show me how it feels to be teased"). These little skits can be done in front of the class, either silently or using words. They can be done individually or in pairs or small groups; refined and practiced or enacted spontaneously.

Curiosity Technique to Try: Classroom Creative Council

Outfit your classroom with a virtual or actual Creative Council—people with a diverse range of expertise in order to generate new thinking and ideas. Casting widely to make creative connections is not a new idea; Thomas Edison gathered people into his own Creative Council for this very reason. It is a practice that has been replicated by many visionaries, inventors and, more recently, innovative companies. That is the thinking in the design of the Hutchins School of Liberal Studies at Sonoma State University, where I teach. Each faculty member has expertise in a different discipline (sociology, literature, history, drama, film, anthropology, psychology, and philosophy, to name a few). When we come together to create an interdisciplinary-themed course, the many perspectives at the table provide all different ways of envisioning the concept.

Have your students imagine a classroom Creative Council of visionaries, inventors, and innovators from our past and present who epitomize the mindsets and dispositions they want to uphold. A Creative Council may be filled with members who everyone in the class has learned about and who we recognize for their individual strengths. Who has a seat on the council is a lesson in itself. Perhaps students can advocate for members and make a case for why their particular perspectives are needed. With one of the members of the Creative Council in mind, we might ask a series of questions and provocations to establish a new point of view about a project or idea. Imagine if Marie Curie or Thomas Edison or Leonardo da Vinci, or any number of other creative visionaries, were in the room. We can tap into their knowledge virtually, by imagining and researching their potential responses and actions. We can ask, "What would _____ think?" or "How would _____ approach this problem?" or "What would _____ say we had forgotten, and why?" In order to answer these questions well, with a depth and authority that allows a new perspective to contribute to our work, we would need to better understand the people involved. The members of our council should be familiar to us, we would need to know their mindset and approach to work and life. Equipped with a deeper knowledge of these role models, we might be able to gain insight from their imaginary mentorship (Barrett, 2015).

In Sum

Imagination and creativity are manifestations of curiosity. Using imagination, children can gain knowledge without needing to have direct experience. Via play, they break down large concepts into smaller units that they can manipulate and explore. Fantasy play serves many functions for learning, including private speech, vocabulary development, flexibility, and self-control. Visceral creative experiences are far better for learning than are virtual ones, because they activate several sensory and brain systems at once. In states of relaxation or daydreaming, improvising or doodling, the creative parts of the brain are most active. Insofar as they activate the imagination, stories can also contribute to the curiosity classroom and enhance learning. The parts of the brain involved in pleasure and those involved in understanding others' perspectives are both activated when we hear stories.

Support Questioning

Questioning belongs at the heart of the curiosity classroom. Effective, critical questioning in students can be developed and taught. It requires patience and faith to let the students set the stage, but nothing is more revealing of their thinking, and nothing is more transformative of their thought processes. According to developmental, cognitive science, and neuroscience research, the absolute best-case scenario for learners is not just to consider and engage with their teachers' questions, but also to cultivate and ask the questions themselves. The way to harness thought, promote inquiry, and scaffold problem solving in the classroom is to transfer as much of the questioning as possible to the students. "Our aim should be to develop in students a lifelong thirst for inquiry and independence in learning. To nurture this spirit in students, teachers need to establish clear inquiry priorities and habits of mind so that thoughtful questions are the norm and students become good questioners" (Rop, 2003, p. 23).

Children's Questions

Asking begins with not knowing and wanting to know. Jean Piaget (1973) called this state disequilibrium. His research in developmental science showed that it was precisely the discomfort of not knowing that puts the child in the mind stance that sets curiosity, seeking, and inquiry in motion. If learning consists of exploring and making sense of things, then questioning is the call to action that ignites learning.

One typical feature of cognitive development is that skills begin by being outwardly expressed before becoming internalized. An example of this is learning to read. We first learn the sounds and how they combine. Next, we sound out the words aloud, and then we begin to read sentences aloud before we are able to internalize the whole process and read quietly in our heads. Children follow the same pattern when they are planning their actions—they use private speech to talk themselves through the steps in a procedure (e.g., "I just need to put this one over here") before gradually shifting the directions to inner thought. In a similar way, being curious and exploring become removed from here and now actions with time (less, "I have to touch this porcelain vase right now" and more, "I love how that porcelain looks. I wonder how it was made. Is it an antique?"). When curiosity becomes internalized, we no longer have to experience something immediately or directly to "get it." We can now wonder about other situations, other places and times, and other people. We can imagine new experiences by reading about them or watching videos about them. The world opens up to us, inviting us to explore via inquiry.

We are so used to children's immense capacity for questions that we take for granted what an amazing set of skills it is (Leslie, 2014). Just as we saw in Chapter 4 on imagination, questioning emerges out of infants' sensory exploration. In-born reflexes jump-start examination. This leads to more general wondering, which leads to checking things out. Children are marvelously, ineffably inquisitive. Asking questions is what children's brains were born to do. For them, seeking explanations is as deeply rooted as seeking food or water (Gopnik, 2009).

Before being able to speak, children use their ability to gesture to ask questions—shrugging shoulders, raising eyebrows, and pointing let their caregivers know what they are curious about (Leslie, 2014). From the time they can talk, children hit the conversational ground asking. A 3- to 5-year-old's questions can range anywhere from wondering, "What's for supper?" to asking about the origins of the universe, ad infinitum. When children encounter something that they do not know or understand, any ambiguity or inconsistency, asking questions allows them to quickly gather information, learn about the world, and solve immediate problems (Chouinard, Harris, & Maratsos, 2007).

Children's questions have been documented and studied as clues to the workings of the developing mind. In these studies, preschoolers were wired with recording devices throughout a typical day at home. The children asked an average of 76 information-seeking questions per hour, both in search of facts and in search of explanations (with one child asking her poor mother 145 questions in a single hour!) (Chouinard et al., 2007). The researchers concluded that "question-asking is a central part of what it means to be a child" (p. 25).

Curiosity Technique to Try: Ask a Hundred Questions

Before a classroom discussion, ask students to generate 100 questions on the topic. For example, if you are reading Roald Dahl's novel *Charlie and the Chocolate Factory*, the students might begin with questioning the events of the story: "Why was Charlie's family so poor?"; "What made Willy Wonka close his doors to outsiders?"; "What if only grown-ups had found the golden tickets?" Then they may begin to ask more analytical questions such as, "Do the Oompa Loompas ever miss Loompaland?"; "What happens if they want to go home?"; "What is the moral of this story?" They might run out of ideas at 20 or 30 questions and begin to get creative or even silly: "What are some things that other magical candies, like the everlasting gobstopper, could do?" And so on. When they really run dry, they can pair up with another student to combine their lists and see how close they can get to 100. The more children get in the habit of asking questions, the more likely they will be to stretch their minds and challenge the texts and people around them.

Questions in School

It is, in fact, nothing short of a miracle that the modern methods of instruction have not yet entirely strangled the holy curiosity of inquiry.

—Albert Einstein

Recent research suggests that entering school can halt student questioning, because schools are top-down enterprises. Teachers tend to ask the questions as a part of guiding the curriculum and pedagogy toward their goals. School districts see it as their responsibility to equip children with a set of frameworks and to fill these frameworks with the necessary content. They use test questions to determine whether or not their predetermined learning goals have been reached. Reasonably enough, most students see it as the teacher's job to ask and their job to answer. When they answer correctly, the logic goes, they have learned something (Greene, 2005). Missing, however, is the inquiring into the frames themselves, and the questioning of the perspective from which things are seen, the ways of thinking, the structures of power, and what is considered OK to question (Opdal, 2001). For example, here are some frame-challenging questions from my own preschool and kindergarten children: "Do birds cough?"; "What happens if God dies?"; "Whose idea was it to make the oceans have salt water?"; "Can teeth bite through teeth?"; "Is love like blood—when you give it does your body make more?"; and "What is the heaviest thing in the world?"

Susan Engel (2011) was interested in understanding what happened to inquisitive preschoolers as they entered kindergarten. She and her team went into elementary schools and noted any time a child asked a question in order to learn more, tinkered with an object, opened something up to look at it, or used other gestures to learn more about something she was interested in. In kindergarten classrooms, episodes of curiosity averaged only about two to five times during any two-hour stretch. By the 5th grade, self-generated questioning was strikingly absent, with an average of zero to two episodes per visit. In other words, most children were spending seven or more hours of their day in school without asking even one question and without taking part in even one behavior aimed at finding out something new (Engel, 2011). While children are natural question askers, whether or not they continue to ask questions and how they channel their inherent curiosity is due in large part to how adults respond to them (Sternberg, 1994).

Questions and Inquiry

All the knowledge we have is a result of asking questions; indeed . . . question asking is the most significant intellectual tool human beings have. Is it not curious, then, that the most significant intellectual skill available to human beings is not taught in school?

—Neil Postman

Questions can be used to further discussion, promote research, prompt summaries or reflection, focus the intelligence of the group, generate a collective emotional perspective, foster shared contexts and joint understandings, offer springboards to new knowledge, invite student participation, encourage talk, present different ways of communicating, or provide a means of handing over control and initiating ownership. They are the chief agents by which meaning and knowledge are mediated (Morgan & Saxton, 2006).

Albert Einstein once said, "If I had an hour to solve a problem and my life depended on the solution, I would spend the first 55 minutes determining the proper question to ask." In his company is a legion of visionaries throughout history (including the likes of Jonas Salk, Jane Goodall, Steve Jobs, and Virginia Woolf) who have attributed their insights to asking the right questions. Recently, a team of researchers set out to understand how innovation and discovery work. They interviewed hundreds of today's top tech geniuses and inventors looking for patterns. As it turned out, these unusual individuals had little in common. The single unifying feature that emerged from the interviews was that every last one of them was skilled in the art of asking great questions (Dyer, Gregersen, & Christensen, 2011).

Questioning belongs in the forefront of pedagogical and curriculum design, since questions both enable and reflect understanding. Student questions are not just portholes into the thoughts that students already have; they are the seeds of thought itself. As philosopher Scott Samuelson has said, "The very act of asking transforms us" (2014, p. 8). For a middle school student to ask a question about a passage that he has read, for example, involves synthesizing the content, finding the line between what is clear and unclear to him using metacognition, tapping into his intrinsic curiosity, and simultaneously articulating and forming thoughts. The reason that teachers claim "There is no such thing as a stupid question" is because students' questions represent their evolving understanding. In short, questioning makes learning visible.

We have all been asking questions since we could talk, but becoming an effective questioner is hard. It takes time and diligence, and the best way to learn about questioning is through questioning (Morgan & Saxton, 2006). This allows students to become active learners who demonstrate ownership of classroom inquiry. "Posing questions . . . must become a habit . . . the questions themselves are far less important than the habit of questioning" (Booth, 2001, p. 210). All of our students need to become skilled at both asking and answering questions.

Sociologist and education visionary Neil Postman believed that the art of question making and asking should be one of the central foci of education. To him, nothing was more basic to intelligence or effective citizenship than learning how to ask productive questions (1979). Good or effective questions require the sort of vitality that challenges students to approach their learning creatively (Morgan & Saxton, 2006). "Questioning breeds actions that lead to further questions, and these, in turn, to the boldness of further inquiring acts" (Kelly, 1963, p. 12). The essence of the question is the opening up and keeping open of possibilities (Gadamer, 1975). Indeed, a good question is seductive; the response it generates is first enjoyment and then analysis. Once children's wonder has been raised, it should be followed up by specific inquiry. There is a lot to wonder about in subjects as diverse as mathematics, physics, and history. By getting to know and by thinking through the concepts, assumptions, and thinking styles that condition one's wonder (metacognition—or being aware of one's own question generating and asking processes), students come to develop perspectives that are more extensive, consistent, and integrative (Opdal, 2001).

Research evidence confirms that the development of questioning in students has hugely positive effects on learning (Dillon, 1983; Dori & Herscovitz, 1999; King, 1994). By asking questions, students become more actively engaged in learning, stimulating cognitive processes and revealing their thinking frameworks. Further, examining a student's questions can be an important indicator of his or her learning. Indeed, behavioral scientists have discovered relationships between students' questioning skills and their performance on Kolb's experiential learning and approaches to learning scale (Pedrosa de Jesus, Almeida, & Watts, 2004; Pedrosa de Jesus, Almeida, Teixeira-Dias, & Watts, 2006).

As they move through elementary, middle, and high school, students often do not feel encouraged to ask questions, either by peers or teachers. In a recent study of the types of questions high school students ask, the vast majority were focused on "doing school," such as, "When did you say this is due?" or "Do we have to know this for the test?" (Carr, 1998). A very small subset of the students' questions was more original and substantive, providing evidence of genuine intellectual curiosity. Classrooms sometimes do have small groups of bright or vocal students who ask questions confidently, are willing to take risks, are willing to interrupt the flow of things, and are not afraid of being wrong (Tobin, 1988). These students are rare, even in classrooms where teachers are running seminar discussions (Dillon, 1983). Middle and high school students ask few questions in class. Typically 80 percent or more of the talking in the classroom is taken up by teacher talk. This creates passive students, tasked with taking in teachers' discursive explanations and answers to questions that they have not asked (Freire, 1998).

Talking at students is the primary way that teachers control what happens in their classroom. Even dialogue in the classroom follows a rather formulaic pattern, where the teacher asks a question either to the whole class or to one particular student and hopes for the right (or at least a good) answer. If the flow is interrupted by an unpredicted curiosity question, teachers tend to answer and then swiftly gain control again by bringing the dyadic sequence back in line (Wertsch & Toma, 1995).

We need to bring questioning pedagogies front and center in our classrooms if we are to promote deep learning. How can we encourage students to pose questions that will strengthen their thinking? What are the conditions that do encourage students to ask questions in school? Professor of science education and curriculum Charles Rop (2003) was interested in those very questions when he set out to examine the students who do ask inquiry questions in school, which he described as follows: (1) The question was related in some way to the content under discussion, (2) the question seemed to originate in student curiosity, and (3) the question was self-described as an attempt to pursue personal inquiry beyond the delivered or expected curriculum. What he discovered was that some students asked questions out of boredom. As one student, Paul, expressed, he wanted to challenge himself to think beyond what was required, "We've got that part, we have it done and then we're going up the ladder and we want to go farther . . . We want more" (Rop, 2003, p. 22). Another student, Kurt, agreed, saying, "We're not satisfied." He explained that doing assignments, memorizing for a test, and writing lab reports were pretty easy to do. He wanted to challenge himself and the teacher and really understand the deeper concepts, "Why does this thing work like this and why doesn't it work like that? Why can't we split an atom in half and keep the energy in light, take the energy and blow up, you know, this table?" (Rop, 2003, p. 23). His teacher's unsatisfying response was simply, 'It just doesn't work that way' (Rop, 2003, p. 23).

Another high school chemistry student, Jeff, explained that he wanted to go deeper into the subject matter than the required understanding, but that his teacher would also put off his questions, either by saying "We can talk about it after class" or "We'll get into that later" (Rop, 2003, p. 24). Jeff and his classmates took such put-offs to mean that the teacher could not spare the time to explain something that was not in the original lesson plan, because of his pressure to cover the entire book during the school year.

Peers also inhibited one another when it came to asking inquiry questions about science. Student perceived that their classmates wanted things to run smoothly, without interruption. This was partly because they wanted to do well on the next test, which was predetermined and still occurred even if they didn't get to cover all of the material. The feeling was that questions take up valuable class time and can hurt test grades. Although they would like things to be different (and they are interested in intellectual growth), these students were resigned to the fact that their personal intellectual questions have little or no place in the classroom, and that school in itself is about doing school-work well. They want to learn deeply and yet they have been educated in a system that requires practical things to trump the essence of learning—they need to know the material for the next exam and for the next course (Rop, 2003). Science teachers, too, want to teach using genuine curiosity and inquiry, but feel guilty—that they are doing their students a disservice and that they will be censured if they do not cover the key content of the discipline. They also will be held accountable for how their students perform on high-stakes state and national proficiency tests. As Tobin explains, "teachers wanting to maintain momentum, smoothness, and group cooperation might actually limit student participation" (1988, p. 318).

On the flip side, when we design our curricula around questioning, we avoid squashing students' inherent wonder, and instead we groom them into intrinsically motivated and inquisitive minds. In the beloved children's novel *Anne of Green Gables*, by L. M. Montgomery, a new teacher comes to town and turns tradition on its head when she encourages the students to ask their questions. Anne is thrilled and instantly engaged: "Mrs. Allan is perfectly lovely . . . She's taken our class and she's a splendid teacher. She said right away she didn't think it was fair for the teacher to ask all the questions, and you know Marilla, that is exactly what I have always thought. She said we could ask her any question we liked, and I asked

Quick Recap

▶ Questioning ignites learning.

▶ Inquiry allows us to explore things outside of the here and now.

▶ Children are voracious questioners.

▶ Entering school often halts children's questioning.

▶ Questions both enable and reflect thinking.

▶ Students report that their own questions are often undervalued in school.

her ever so many. I'm good at asking questions" (Montgomery, 1908/1976, p. 238). Indeed, the transformative power of curiosity is the basis for a dynamic classroom with students who are propelled by questions and seeking to understand. When we stimulate questions and critical reflection about the questions (asking students what they mean by their questions), we catapult their curiosity (Freire, 1998). Checking things out, being curious, wondering, systematically exploring and experimenting, asking, and seeking answers are the essential ingredients for learning. These should be our primary concern in the classroom. If these initial conditions are satisfied, we will never have to work hard for learning to occur again.

Curiosity Technique to Try: Object-Based Learning

German educator Friedrich Froebel (who is best known as the father of kindergarten) revolutionized early education in the 1840s when he gave students open-ended physical objects and manipulatives to guide their learning (Curtis & Carter, 2015). Objects can be used both as a means of generating questions and as a vehicle for understanding the content of a lesson. When you provoke curiosity using objects (like collections of geodes or watch parts or antique tools or sea shells) students are put in a natural questioning position. Seeing something new or unusual on the desk in front of them, they can't help but wonder, "What are these things? What do they do?" In this way, object-based lessons use things to help children discover new information by provoking them to pose and investigate their own questions. Students are also led to their own answers, as their teachers respond to inquiry with further open-ended questions and return their focus to the object itself. In object-based learning, new understanding truly follows the paths forged by the students (Alvarado & Herr, 2003).

Begin an object-based lesson by simply placing an object in the center of each table. In the Birds of a Feather science lesson plan, the goal is to lead students to the understanding that characteristics of feathers can lead us to discover the distinct differences between birds, in particular, how they have adapted to their needs to obtain food (Alvarado & Herr, 2003). Arrange the class into pairs and give each pair a feather from the collection. Students love handling real feathers and enjoy observing them and recording their observations. They should record the weight, length, width at widest point, and colors of their feather. Then they should predict what kind of bird their feather came from, being careful to include concrete reasons why they believe that it came from that bird. When they present their predictions to the class, peers can ask further questions or make suggestions to help with the next steps. Then, ask the students to generate 10 questions that they would like answered about their feather or the bird it came from. Now, they should research their feather and try to find out what bird it came from, using evidence to support their findings (Alvarado & Herr, 2003).

If your students become overwhelmed or antsy to find answers during the question-generating phase, ask them some guiding questions to help them along, such as, "Are all feathers on a bird alike? Does the size of the feather fit the size of the bird you think it came from? What does your feather tell you about the habits of the bird? How is your feather different from the other feathers?" (Alvarado & Herr, 2003, p. 98). Be sure to avoid just giving them answers. Remember, the inquiry process itself is the most valuable part of this lesson.

Question Frameworks: Divergent Thinking

Children love to inquire about those things we normally take for granted. Whereas adult philosophers tend to assume the rules are binding, children know of few such responsibilities. For this reason, children will be more inclined toward wonder, and they will notice peculiarities and possibilities overlooked by the rest of us (Opdal, 2001). This capacity translates into the ability to question the foundations and frameworks of thinking itself. There are many things that the child may have thought about or noticed that would most certainly elude the adult. We can only know their thinking by accessing it before tampering with it. Even after spending every day with them, I am still always surprised by my children's understanding of things—their sense of reality, which seems at first glance to correspond with mine, is revealed as vastly different when I simply ask their perspective. Questions like "Can Nanny be in two places at one time?" or "Can pretend things still have feelings?" or "Who made the earth? Was it Martin Luther King Jr.?" reveal the ways in which my daughter Sonia's world is a completely mysterious and open place, with few boundaries.

Saahil Roy stared at the puzzle on his desk: nine dots in three rows with the instructions to draw four straight lines to connect them. He had been staring at it for 40 minutes, and kept feeling like he was going to get it, but then saw the rule that the pencil could not be lifted from the paper. "It's not possible," he finally said aloud, prompting his 6-year-old son, Rahal, to enter the room. "Start here, Papa," Rahal said, his pencil literally outside of the box. In five minutes and four quick lines, forming an arrow-like image, Rahal had solved the puzzle (see Figure 1). Of course, how silly that he hadn't thought of that before! Saahil was embarrassed by how limited he had been by an artificial boundary.

Children are more likely than adults to use innovative and creative ways to solve problems. This is because children are more flexible learners than adults. They can quickly come to discover relationships between abstract objects and then apply those rules to make inferences about brand-new events. For instance, in one experiment, 4-year-olds and adults were asked to figure out which objects were causing a reaction and then classify new

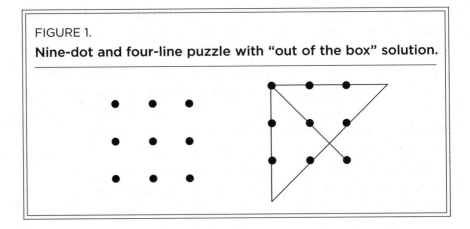

FIGURE 1.

Nine-dot and four-line puzzle with "out of the box" solution.

objects based on the pattern. The 4-year-olds significantly outperformed the adults because they were better at learning causal relationships and principles that went against their prior experience. Children can quickly assimilate new information, even counterintuitive information, and integrate that into their decision-making repertoires. They can also seamlessly update their beliefs to understand completely new ways of seeing and doing things. Fewer entrenched ideas equates to superior flexibility across domains. The fact that children know less, ironically, makes them better (or at least more unbiased) learners. Such malleability of early beliefs seems to underlie the "bold exploration and breathtaking innovation" that characterizes children's learning (Lucas, Bridgers, Griffiths, & Gopnik, 2014, p. 297).

Children are also superior to adults in the ability to find creative or unusual, non-scripted, solutions to problems. Divergent thinkers often reframe or expand the scope of a problem, see it in a new way, make connections that may be not be obvious, reach solutions beyond the logical, and even "dream the impossible" (Carnevale, Gainer, & Meltzer, 1990, p. 201). Their orientation to problems can make the unfeasible a delightful reality. Divergent thinkers tend to be makers and creators, innovators, artists, and those who make big changes in the world. They reach beyond artificial limits and come up with innovative ideas even at the risk of failing.

What is interesting about divergent thinking is that it is highly valued in the adult world (e.g., a recent survey of thousands of CEOs from 33 different industries called divergent thinking the factor most critical for success), and yet, it is not taught in schools (Pappano, 2014). Children are natural divergent thinkers. In a now classic series of studies, systems scientist George Land gave tests of divergent thinking to more than 1,000 children. The tests were identical to those that he had given to help NASA select scientists and engineers, with open-ended questions such as, "How are a potato and carrot alike?" or "How many uses can you find for a paperclip?" (Land & Jarman, 1993). Scored for originality of responses, the results looked like this: In 3- to 5-year-olds, 98 percent of those tested scored in the top tier—a level they called "creative genius." When the very same group of kids was tested five years later, only 32 percent scored in this top tier. After another five years, only 10 percent of the same kids scored in the top tier. More than 280,000 adults have taken the same set of tests, and only 2 percent have scored in the top tier (Naiman, 2014).

In a profound set of experiments, teams of kindergarten children competed against teams of Harvard MBA graduate students to build the tallest tower possible under a strict time limit, using only uncooked sticks of spaghetti, string, tape, and a marshmallow. The MBA students tended toward planning and approaching the problem analytically, but when their structures fell apart they did not leave enough time to rebuild. Kindergartners used the time much more efficiently by building right away. They made significantly more attempts rather than trying to get it right the first time. The kindergartners also learned from their mistakes in real time (Berger, 2014). As Sutton (2009) has pointed out, the most highly successful thinkers (scientists, composers, artists, and authors) experience the greatest number of failures, because they make the most attempts. There is little evidence that they are more often successful in their endeavors. They simply make more tries.

Quick Recap

▶ Children often notice details and possibilities that elude adults.

▶ Children are more likely than adults to use divergent thinking to solve problems.

▶ Divergent thinking is highly valued in the adult world, yet rarely taught or acknowledged in school.

▶ The best thinkers and problem solvers are not the most successful; they simply make the most attempts.

Curiosity Technique to Try: Break Things to Understand Them

Ever the social and technological innovators, Google's education division has begun setting up breaking centers to teach children about what things are made of and how they are designed. They also learn a thing or two about physics and environmental and waste management. In the Google Breaker Lab, children get to use their divergent thinking skills to pick out an object to smash, perhaps a clay pot, ceramic dolphin, keyboard from a 1990s computer, or outdated remote control. The item is then placed in a glass case and broken using various means (Google likes to have children jump on a platform to create the pressure for two metal plates to squish the items until they break, but you can simply put them in a box and crush them with something heavy). If you have a clear box, you can film the breakage and play it back in slow motion. Or just collect the pieces on a tray to be examined afterwards. Like any laboratory experience, the Breaker Lab should involve performing background research, forming hypotheses, integrating scientific principles, and going back to revise theories based on the evidence from the data. But unlike traditional science lab assignments, its divergent counterintuitive nature makes it almost endlessly interesting for children, thus likely to provoke many attempts at breaking and understanding.

The Practice of Asking

Children enter school as animated interrogation points, and instead of having their mental hunger gratified, they are stuffed with knowledge they have not asked for, and required to answer instead of being led to question, until their intellectual appetite is dulled . . . It is not the truth they are after, but the words and acts that will satisfy the teacher.

—Edwin Kirkpatrick, *Fundamentals of Child Study*

Can we keep students' inherent curiosity and learning wedded together throughout their formal education? Unfortunately, "banking education," the transmission of information by the teacher to passive students who receive and are expected to regurgitate that information, has been the dominant experience of most of our students (Freire, 2000). Whereas engaged living is a process of curiosity, engaged education is a process of inquiry. We educators must make it our goal to direct children's wonder into a method or learning process (Opdal, 2001). Questions are an important part of that process. They emphasize and support a habit of mind—the love of learning—which is transferrable beyond a particular content.

Yet, although we extol the virtues of creativity and insight in learners, questioning—the engine of transformative and critical thinking—is rarely taught or even rewarded in school. In school, from preK through higher education, questions tend to come from the teacher. These questions are often designed to get students thinking, perhaps to open up their minds and to provide analysis of the content at hand. Teachers' questions, at their best, can be an invitation to challenge one's assumptions, engage, integrate, and join larger dialogues. They can model creative and critical ways of examining the material. But even at their most inspiring, teachers' questions function to guide students' thinking along some predetermined path. They are ultimately designed to elicit correct answers (or at least answers within a certain specified and appropriate framework of thinking).

Genuine questioning involves much more than generating answers. It is a pattern of behavior—a way of being—that forges new paths and challenges assumptions that may otherwise be taken for granted. A student who has developed into a questioner will wonder, "Why are we doing this particular thing in this particular way?" (Berger, 2014, p. 2). Habitual questioners have "the ability to go to a poem, a painting, a piece of music—or a document, a mathematical description, a science experiment—and locate a novel direction for investigation" (Wolf, 1987, p. 7). If we educators are interested in deep and lasting student learning (including the connected habits of mind of creativity, innovation, and critique), then we need to go beyond that first step of posing interesting questions to our students. Our end goal must be to teach our students how to develop and articulate their own questions, and while they are at it, to question everything around them.

The most powerful learning occurs when students ask the questions, for several reasons. First, when students ask the questions, intrinsic motivation is ignited. Asking their own sincere questions (those they are genuinely interested in knowing; those they cannot stop thinking about) activates that internal desire for action, intrinsic motivation. Studies show that questions only become genuine areas of inquiry for students when they ask them themselves (Cifone, 2013). Second, when students ask the questions, the prefrontal cortex of the brain is activated. The prefrontal cortex is responsible for the combined questioning and critical thinking that underlie inquiry (Gupta, 2012).

Third, whoever asks the questions holds the power. When students ask the questions, the classroom social dynamic is changed from top-down to bottom-up. Teacher-initiated questions implicitly let the students know the boundaries of what can be examined, setting up a top-down power dynamic. If those in power are setting up the discourse, then they are limiting the bounds of knowledge, often without even realizing it (Foucault, 1982, p. 218). Indeed, when Brown University professor Dennie Palmer Wolf (1987) recorded episodes of questioning in schools, she discovered that teachers tended to monopolize the right to question, ceding power only to select few bright, privileged students. At alternative schools designed around inquiry, like Brightworks High School in San Francisco, the standard curriculum is reframed with questions such as, "What is interesting to you?"—a question that surprisingly few high school students have ever been asked (Goyal, 2012). Constructing their own questions challenges students to approach their learning more creatively. It also breeds further questions and the boldness of more inquiring acts, opening up and keeping open possibilities (Morgan & Saxton, 2006).

Fourth, when students ask the questions, they manipulate—and thus remember—ideas and concepts. Remembering information is not the same as constructing knowledge. When it comes to learning, the facts and tidbits that are useful on tests are rarely useful once one goes outside the classroom walls. Questioning is by nature active. When we are forced to form and articulate our questions, we are being asked to do something with the information at hand: to apply it and think about it. Learning involves research and personal inquiry, and develops through doing. According Dewey, "When the feeling of a genuine perplexity lays hold of any mind (no matter how the feeling arises), that mind is alert and inquiring, because stimulated from within" (1909, p. 336). We remember what we ourselves wondered in school, and continue to wonder.

Student questions are not just portholes into the thoughts that they already have; their questions are the seeds of thought itself. For a middle school student to ask about a passage that she has read, for example, involves synthesizing the content, finding the line between what is clear and unclear to her (i.e., metacognition), tapping into her intrinsic curiosity, and simultaneously articulating and forming thoughts. Her questions about the passage both enable and reflect her emerging understanding. There is a tradition in composition education in which students "write to learn," or discover as they go. There should also be a tradition of "asking to learn," where students articulate and at the same time develop their thinking as they question (Ostroff, 2015). Indeed, when students are instructed to brainstorm using only questions, as opposed to more fully formed thoughts, imagination opens up like a floodgate, with ideas becoming creative, subversive, playful, and filled with possibility (Berger, 2014).

I would have little idea where my students are intellectually if I merely asked them *my questions* about the topics we are examining. Their questions reveal to me not just what they understood from the particular text or experience. They bring to the surface the many facets of their developing learning process: clear ideas about what they want to find out; less well-developed ideas that they need to figure out; attempts to find out what might work; and ultimately, their personal discourse with themselves. My students' own questions reveal their assumptions, frameworks, and realities. They expose their biases and my own biases. They allow me to see what is being taken for granted and what might be possible (Ostroff, 2015).

Asking a question doesn't only make my students' learning explicit to me, it also makes their learning and thinking explicit to themselves. In other words, it enhances their metacognition. Metacognition is the process of thinking about one's own thinking. Understanding and owning the process of learning via metacognition propels the learning itself (Ostroff, 2012). Children who ask themselves about their understanding while they read comprehend books better than those who do not (Rumelhart, 1991; Trabasso & Suh, 1993). Likewise, students in the habit of explaining and challenging science textbook passages as they studied better understood the scientific principles over time (Chi, Bassock, Lewis, Reimann, & Glaser, 1989). In short, questioning is an effective tool for metacognition, since it makes learning visible, both to the learner him- or herself and to the teacher-learner guiding the process.

The absolute best-case scenario for learning is not just being able to consider and engage with teachers' questions,

Quick Recap

▶ Being curious and asking questions primes our brains to learn.

▶ Inquiry should be a major focus in education.

▶ Questioning is rarely taught or even rewarded in school.

▶ Whoever asks the questions holds the power over the discourse—in school, the teachers tend to ask the questions.

▶ The most powerful learning occurs when students ask the questions.

but to ask them. Students construct knowledge more effectively when their own questions drive their learning, and great question asking skills can be taught. Given the opportunity, students can learn to generate a range of different types of questions, figure out which ones will be the most fruitful to them and why, and strategize how to effectively use them (Rothstein & Santana, 2011).

Curiosity Technique to Try: Question Formulation Technique (QFT)

Desperately seeking to ignite the enthusiasm and curiosity in their students, teachers regularly add to their already heavy workload by trying to figure out prompts and questions that will unleash student creativity and problem-solving abilities. But letting the students ask the questions is even better.

Educators and activists Dan Rothstein and Luz Santana (2011) have created and rigorously tested a student-driven questioning technique called the Question Formulation Technique (QFT), which is done in six steps. First, the teacher puts out a Question Focus (Q Focus), a focused theme or topic that will be the jumping-off point for the students' own questions. An effective Q Focus will both provoke and stimulate new lines of thinking, something like, The Inside of a Cell, Defeating Math Anxiety, or Defining What Is Natural. Next, the students form groups of three to five students and begin to produce questions for about five minutes according to some simple rules:

1. Ask as many questions as you can.
2. Do not stop to discuss, judge, or answer any question. Merely write down every question exactly as it is stated.
3. Change statements that come up into questions.

Next, the students improve their questions. One way to do this is to spend some time beforehand on open-ended versus closed-ended questions. Remind students that these types of questions have different functions and that both can be useful. (Open-ended questions tend to start with "Why?" or "How?" while closed-ended questions tend to start with "Is?", "Do?", or "Can?"). During the question improvement phase, the students should rate each question as open- or closed-ended (O or C) and then practice changing a few Cs to Os and Os to Cs. For example, the closed-ended question, "When can we have free time during the school day to work on our projects?" could be changed to, "What time of day would be most effective as a free period to work on our projects?" (Rothstein & Santana, 2011).

The students then select their priority questions—the three best from their list. They may choose the three that most interest them, are most important, would help them best to discuss the text, or best relate to the Q Focus, depending on the focus of your lesson. After making their choices, they should provide a rationale for their choices. Students and teacher should work together to plan how they will use their priority questions. At the end of the unit, students should reflect on what they have learned, how they learned it, and how they will use it (Rothstein & Santana, 2011).

Boston-area high school humanities teacher Ling-Se Peet had great success with the QFT. She began the lesson with the Q-Focus Torture Can Be Justified. One student group focused their questions on defining torture and understanding its meaning and limits. Another group focused more specifically on the Q Focus: In what situations should torture be used? Or the more specific, Why is torture effective? Students reported that being able to change the questions made them feel more confident asking and figuring out how to solve problems for themselves. They gained experience using their own questions to debate, discuss, assess, and prioritize. In other words, these high school humanities students had set their own agenda of what they wanted to know (Rothstein & Santana, 2011).

About the QFT process, history teacher Laurie Gaughran commented,

> When [my students] submit a paper to me, and I want them to think more about it, I go ahead and list all kinds of questions— writing on the margins of their papers—to get them to think about it all. But the QFT is pushing me to see that it would be better if they could look at their own work and learn to ask the kinds of questions I'm asking and some I am not thinking about. (Rothstein & Santana, 2011, p. 9)

The Socratic Method

It is not just the held facts, retrievable knowledge, or demonstrable skills that determine whether one is truly educated, the real test is in the development of a spirit of thoughtful curiosity and the disciplined habits of inquiry to support it.

> —Charles J. Rop, "Spontaneous Inquiry Questions in
> High School Chemistry Classrooms," in
> *International Journal of Science Education*

To understand the lasting power of questioning, we need to go back almost 2,500 years to Athens, Greece. Traveling scholars called the Sophists went from town to town educating wealthy youth. They claimed to teach excellence and virtue to young noblemen and demanded pricey fees for their lessons. The Sophists were considered savvy in winning arguments, and their mode of education was to impart their students with their expert knowledge (Stewart, 2012).

In contrast, the revolutionary philosopher and teacher Socrates presented himself to his students not as a master of understanding but as a fellow questioner working toward the discovery of truth. His method of teaching was to walk around and engage people in an informal dialogue. He would claim not to know anything himself, and because of that humility, people would let their guard down. Socrates would then ask questions to help the students think for themselves and search for a deeper truth. He was skilled at asking just the right questions to force self-examination, unravel assumptions, and get his students to think and rethink their insights and perspectives. Socrates made people think more deeply about their ideas. His goal was to wake people up from their dogmatic slumber so that they could face their areas of uncertainty and search for the truth (Bedell, 1980).

Socrates's discussions were an unusual pedagogy in that no definitive knowledge ever came from them. The learning outcome was not a concrete set of content, but rather the increased tendency for his students to call into question what they saw before themselves. Ironically, non-action on the part of Socrates had the strange effect of making his pupils very active. Socrates described himself as an "intellectual midwife, whose questioning delivers the thoughts of others into the light of day" (Stewart, 2012). He played the role of the humble inquirer—and even pretended to be ignorant. The fact that Socrates expressed a genuine equality with pupils led them to feel empowered. They became free to question the logic and ideas of the instructor, as well as to question themselves. As a result, both the teacher and student were better able to order their thoughts and arguments into stronger, more coherent theories (Stewart, 2012).

Socratic dialogue is used today when educators create space for students to engage in co-thinking and self-directed learning and to uncover what is true for them as individuals and as a group. In a Socratic seminar, teachers do not play the role of the expert or the authority. Instead they guide the classroom according to what direction begins to yield the most understanding, clarification, or insight (Stein, 1991). Socratic questioning is disciplined questioning that can be used to pursue thought in many directions: to explore complex ideas, get to the truth of things, open up issues and problems, uncover assumptions, analyze concepts, distinguish what is known from what is not known, and follow out logical implications of thought (Paul & Elder, 2007). Socrates has shown us that by questioning all things (own biases especially) we can arrive at critical thinking and knowing.

A good Socratic seminar begins and ends with questions. In the beginning questions are often for understanding, but then deeper questions begin to emerge; critical questions that are genuine—coming from the participants themselves. Questions towards the end of each Socratic seminar should focus on synthesizing ideas (e.g., "What have been the highlights? What have been the rough spots?"; "What do we now understand? What do we still not understand?"), and on the process of dialogue itself (e.g., "Whose voices didn't we hear? Why?") (Wiggins, 2013).

Quick Recap

▶ Greek philosopher Socrates was skilled at asking questions, which got his students to challenge their own assumptions and think deeper.

▶ In a Socratic seminar, the teacher does not impart knowledge but rather guides the group in dialogue to think critically and question all things.

▶ Socratic seminars unearth content and insights, but they should also include reflection on the process of dialogue.

Curiosity Technique to Try: Use the Five Whys to Solve Classroom Problems

The Five Whys is a discussion-based, problem-solving technique that was developed by Japanese inventor Sakichi Toyoda. The concept is simple: When something goes wrong, we tend to seek to blame someone. A much more adaptive way is to see it as a learning opportunity and use inquiry to excavate the situation. Asking questions and dialoging about the problem can help us to see the root causes of it and to change our understanding of it. This method is based on the philosophy that people do not fail, processes fail (Berger, 2014).

As an example, let's say that it becomes apparent that your students are not prepared for class and that very few of them have read the book. Instead of getting mad and giving pop quizzes or other punishment, you can ask five why questions to try to determine why this is happening and what can be done about it:

Problem: The students have not read the book and are not prepared for class.

Why? They had too much other work for other classes.

Why? All of their teachers assigned big projects at the same time, around mid-term.

Why? The parent open house is approaching, and teachers want to be sure that they have enough student work to showcase.

Why? Parents need to see concrete achievements.

Why? Parent-teacher meetings are only 10 minutes long, which is not enough time to go into the nuances how each child is learning.

Proposed solutions: Extend parent-teacher meetings to 30 minutes. Encourage teachers to post major assignment due dates to a central calendar to encourage greater staggering. Implement assessment portfolios that include self-reflection and self-assessment and allow parents to understand their child's learning as a process, not just a product.

In Sum

Questions are curiosity writ large. They allow students to discover, build upon, and reveal their thinking, fueling the fires of intellect. The act of asking activates the prefrontal cortex, also known as the critical thinking part of the brain. Questioning engages students more deeply in their learning and fosters the internal manipulation (thus remembering) of complex concepts and ideas.

Young children are champion questioners—by 2 or 3 years old, curious children have been known to ask hundreds of questions per hour. But when they enter formal school, their questions rapidly diminish, largely due to a historical precedent that it is the teachers who ask the questions. If we want to support divergent thinking and creative problem solving, we need to begin teaching and rewarding question asking throughout formal education. Socratic seminar discussions are a best practice for engaging students in inquiry and collaboration, and they are an effective mode of learning from kindergarten through higher education. After all, asking, re-asking, refining, and thinking through one's own authentic questions are essential steps on the path to lifelong learning.

Make Time

> *Do I dare set forth here the most important, the most useful rule of all education? It is not to save time, but to squander it.*
>
> —Jean-Jacques Rousseau, *Emile*

We have found ourselves in a great hurry. Even in child care at age 2, the toddlers are practicing, so that next year in preschool, they will be able to sit still through circle time. And the preschool students are gearing up for success in kindergarten. Elementary school kids hear almost daily about the real pressures that lie on the horizon of middle school. High school is, of course, where students must acquire the skills and achieve the grades if they even want to be considered for a decent college. Undergraduate is the time to get the experience needed to get into grad school or medical school or law school. Unless your record is impeccable and you have prepared, the prevailing wisdom goes, you will not succeed.

On the scale of the individual school day, there is an almost endless amount of work to be done. Teachers have to hit all of the learning outcomes on the lesson plans, which have to map on to all of the content standards. Prep time is only 40 minutes long for the week, and lesson plans are due for the following week. Kindergartners have 10 minutes left in centers to complete their pumpkin craft project, do the subtraction worksheet, and meet with reading buddies, before being asked to transition into snack or circle time. District assessments and standardized testing are beginning in three days, and we have not come close to finishing the unit on the periodic table, or Shakespeare, or fractions.

The prevailing cultural myth of our era is that we are forever short on time. And that feeds into corollary myths: that educators must prioritize content rather than build understanding in order to prepare students for success on examinations and tests; that quantifiable achievement trumps slowing down and genuinely engaging (McRobbie & Tobin, 1997). Even when we are doing something we value, like reading a book to our students, a part of us is ready to run to the next thing, channelsurfing our very lives (Samuelson, 2014). But transitions can be extremely stressful on the attentional systems of the brain, especially for young children. Our frantic pace in the classroom (e.g., "Now it's snack time!"; "Now it's clean up time!"; "Sit down and work on math skills!"; "Pay attention to me, we have five minutes before PE!") may in fact be setting children up for the attention deficit epidemic we claim is their fault. If we are to engage and approach the material as a community of learners, we must learn when to deviate from the plan and to go through the slower, more nurturing, and more ephemeral processes of understanding.

In the storybook *Frog and Toad Together*, by Arnold Lobel, Frog has grown a beautiful garden and Toad, very impressed and a little bit jealous, wants to grow one, too. Frog gives him some seeds, and Toad plans to immediately plant them, water them, and reap the results. He sits and sits and waits for them to grow. Toad begins to walk around the rows and tell his seeds in no uncertain terms, "Now seeds start growing." When they don't immediately respond, Toad gets increasingly impatient. He is frustrated and pacing and shouting at the seeds, "Now seeds start growing!" Frog hears this terrible racket and comes over. "Toad," he says gently, "these poor seeds are afraid to grow!" What Toad needs to do is to spend the time. He needs to nurture the seeds gently. So Toad begins playing the violin for his seeds and reading them stories. He recites poetry for them and sits with them when it rains. And just when Toad falls fast asleep in his labor, the little nurtured seeds begin to emerge. Just like Toad, we need to change our rushed-for-outcomes model and begin listening to our students' own rhythms in order to help them grow.

Recent research suggests that teachers' experience of intense time constraints (coupled with pressure to conform to the heavy content load of the state and national curriculum) means restricting meaningful discussion and student intellectual involvement (Newton, Driver, & Osborne, 1999). One kindergarten teacher lamented, "My students come in and play for about 20 minutes every morning. There have been many mornings this year that I have sat back and just observed. They were SO engaged and playing cooperatively that I would say to my aide, 'I just wish I could let them keep doing this all day!' Unfortunately I can only afford to give them about 10–15 extra minutes before we need to start our day crammed with lessons around the state standards."

Most teachers want to engage their students in free discourse, really delve into questions and curiosities, and be flexible on the instruction methods and content covered, but that flexibility poses a dilemma for the teacher. How can she justify two valuable weeks away from the school's prescribed curriculum, when, at the end of the day, she will be held accountable for that missed content (Yerrick, 2000)? If the students do not perform well, her job may even be on the line.

If we step back and examine the way the brain learns, and if we reorient our goals toward creating the curiosity classroom, we will discover that rushing is not the path to deep learning. A quarter of a century of research on literacy, for instance, has shown that reading levels skyrocket when students are given choices of books and the time to get lost in them (Atwell, 2015). I recently conducted a survey of teachers and asked them, "If you could invent your own school, and had unlimited academic freedom and resources, what three things would you change first about how the school day is spent?" The results were astonishing (and almost unheard of in the realm of social science research). One hundred percent of my respondents, *every single teacher*, named time as one of the three things they would change if they were given the power. Teachers said they would implement longer individual class times or just one subject per day, quiet time for mindful reflection, and the freedom to determine how things play out, regardless of what the lesson plan intended. Kindergarten teacher Leah Amaru said that she would schedule much more time outside, as well as significantly more time on multi-sensory curriculum; 4th grade teacher Susan Ruckle would eliminate all scheduling and allow for extra time to expand the lesson if and when the kids are interested; high school math teacher LaToya Hamilton would let her students decide how they would like to spend their day and then hold them accountable for accomplishing their individual goals on their own schedules.

Our Relationship to Time

One common fear of new teachers is classroom management. How on earth, my students—who are prospective teachers—ask, am I going to keep a classroom of 27 children with varying attention spans occupied so that they don't cause trouble? Scheduling every second of the day seems like a foolproof solution to that problem. We have been told since the time of St. Augustine that idle hands do the devil's work. But curiosity requires some idling. It takes us from our tasks and goals, making us abandon what we are supposed to be doing to follow the mysteries that spontaneously present themselves (Leslie, 2014). But if we can create a culture of exploration and engagement, intrinsic motivation will be high, which effectively removes the problem of misbehavior. The curiosity classroom relies upon fluidity and possibility for surprise and openness.

In one study, highly motivated high school students reported that classroom timeframes were impeding their genuine and spontaneous inquiry (Rop, 2003). Some students, like Jeff, felt that the pace of the lessons was too slow. He complained that everything in his physical science class had been a review of material they covered the previous year. Jeff tried to up the ante intellectually by asking tough questions but was met with resistance from both teachers and peers (Rop, 2003). It seemed that his teachers wanted to move on with their own agendas. Jeff's classmates shunned him, worried that the material on the upcoming test would not be covered sufficiently if time was taken out to address his questions. Engaged students who would like more than they are being offered are often met with the "put off," which means that the teacher is so busy pushing content that he dodges a genuine question. Sample versions of the put off include being told, "We'll get to that later" or "Oh, I don't have time to explain it right now." Motivated students interpret that response to mean that their questions are inappropriate or beyond the teacher's agenda, which (cultural mores tell us) always trumps the student's agenda. Another student in this study, Kurt, said he understood that teachers are perennially short on time and need to keep on task so they can cover a huge amount of content. According to Kurt, there just is not time for students' genuine interest. "They're pressed for time and so they just gotta crunch it in. They say things like, 'We need to push on because there is so much to do. I would love to be able to go into that, but, you know, this really should be a two-year course'" (Rop, 2003, p. 26). Similarly, a recent review of advanced placement courses in mathematics and science by the National Science Foundation and the U.S. Department of Education reported that most AP courses crammed in too much material in too short a time, at the expense of understanding (Holt, 2002). To make curiosity a priority, we must slow down, and make space for the true spirit of inquiry (Rop, 2003).

Quick Recap

▶ Rushing is not the path to deep learning.

▶ Transitions can be stressful on the attention systems of children's brains.

▶ When students are genuinely engaged, classroom management concerns dwindle.

▶ Boredom can be stressful, but transcending boredom is empowering and creativity inducing.

Vary the Learning Situation

Authentic learning is quite variable when it comes to pacing. Sometimes curiosity might be mosquito-like, dancing from idea to idea in an excited frenzy, and sometimes it may be more slow and wandering. Deep learning that comes from genuine curiosity is never forced, because it originates from the learner. Curiosity does not hold up well under impatience. Teachers need to be empowered to slow down and provide students time to wonder and be curious. We must also give time and free rein to the ever curious and questioning students; we must let them exist within that heightened state of hungering for knowledge (Shonstrom, 2014). How can the amorphous learning process be documented and prioritized over the product?

Here we can take a lesson from education models that emphasize larger frames of time and swaths of freedom within a variety of modes of instruction. Pediatrician and pedagogue Maria Montessori meticulously observed children for many years before developing her education model. One of Montessori's most interesting discoveries was that frequent changes in what the child was working on caused greater fatigue than did continuous work of one kind. It turned out that it was exhausting to keep switching gears, and when children were left alone for a nice long chunk of time to work at their own pace, attention and engagement skyrocketed. For children who needed or wanted a break, the freedom to take a break was there, but it was self-selected. (When the timing was externally imposed, on the other hand, breaks could be exhaustive and disruptive.) A child as young as 3, having spent a few months in the Montessori classroom, was able to choose challenging work, focus on the task at hand, finish a cycle of work, rest without interrupting those who are working, and repeat this sequence. Montessori's meticulous documentation of the learning process showed that for this to happen, a minimum of three hours of uninterrupted classroom time was essential. Observing uninterrupted children, Montessori noted, "Each time a polarization of attention took place, the child began to be completely transformed, to become calmer, more intelligent, and more expansive" (1989, p. 21). True learning and development cannot happen in 20-minute spurts (Lillard, 2005). When children know that they are about to be interrupted, at best they choose less challenging "busywork" and at worst become nuisances to their peers. Even more tragic, when children do not know an interruption is coming, they choose demanding work and become engrossed, but then are blindsided and derailed when the disruption takes place (Lillard, 2005).

How can the teacher cover all of the requirements and still allow for longer blocks of time? This is only possible when we change the way we think about teaching and learning. According to Montessori, "Our aim therefore is not merely to make the child understand . . . but to so touch his imagination as to enthuse him to his inmost core. We do not want complacent pupils, but eager ones" (1989, p. 11). She believed that "the child should love everything he learns" (Montessori, 1989, p. 17). When the learning materials and pedagogy are carefully designed with the self-guided learner in mind, the child's drive for knowledge and the material's self-correcting qualities are the true teachers—the adult just brings the child and the material together as a kind of middleman of the learning process. Research showed that children at a public, inner-city Montessori school significantly outperformed their peers at traditional schools in both cognitive/academic measures and social/behavioral measures. In particular, 5-year-olds in Montessori showed higher achievement in academic skills related to school readiness like letter word identification, phonetic decoding, applied math problem-solving skills, and executive function skills. They also performed better on measures of theory of mind, social cognition, classroom ethics and justice, and positive shared play. Twelve-year-olds in Montessori outperformed peers in sophisticated sentence structures, creative story writing, positive social strategies, and sense of school community (Lillard & Else-Quest, 2006). It might just be that the time spent and avoidance of the time pressure has something to do with these results.

Slow Schools

Pockets of educators are beginning to realize that genuine learning does not occur against the clock. Similarly, authentic curiosity grows in fits, starts, and unpredictable leaps. According to child development experts Roberta Golinkoff and Kathy Hirsh-Pasek (2003), one of our greatest misconceptions when it comes to teaching children is the belief that "faster is better" and that we must "make every moment count." According to the research evidence, the message is clear: Children learn best when they are relaxed, less regimented, and less hurried. In the same spirit, the dean of Harvard College advised his incoming class of super-achiever students to take the slow road to learning by not spending all of their time studying, but instead allowing themselves unstructured time each day. He said, "Empty time is not a vacuum to be filled: it is the thing that enables the other things on your mind to be creatively rearranged, like the empty square in the 4×4 puzzle which makes it possible to move the other 15 pieces around" (Lewis, 2001, p. 5). Even the national education system of Japan (which was once known for its machine-like precision and efficiency) has been radically changed, allowing students much more free time. Ken Terawaki, senior official of the Japanese Ministry of Education, explained, "Our current system, just telling kids to study, study, study, has been a failure. Endless study worked in the past, but that is no longer the case . . . We want to give them some time to think" (Holt, 2002, p. 10). Japanese educators have discovered that an unimaginative and orderly school system produces disciplined workers, but not problem solvers and innovators for the future (French, 2001).

Just as the Slow Food Movement has questioned the cultural dignity lost to speed, efficiency, and convenience of fast food chains, the Slow Schools Movement eschews rushed educational practice with imposed content and sequence, which is assessed via agreed-upon ends capable of numerical expression (Holt, 2002). Rather than delivering knowledge and skills, cutting costs, standardizing resources, and rushing teachers through their boring scripts and routines, slow schools seek to equip their teachers and students with the abilities to creatively address the unpredictable problems of life, engage with a world of growing subtlety and complexity, and let themselves grow as authentically curious individuals. Exactly as it is more satisfying to eat one wild caught salmon fillet than three super-sized burgers, students will be more gratified by understanding the reasons why Alexander Hamilton stood up for a strong federal government than by memorizing the capitals of the 50 states. When a student takes the time to understand (rather than to just "cover") what Newton's concepts of mass and force imply, to appreciate them in all of their abstract elegance and cultural context, the algorithms will be understood seamlessly (Holt, 2002). In an unrushed school, the seeds of lifelong curiosity are sown.

Curiosity Technique to Try:
Mixed and Individualized Pacing

How can individualized and variable pacing be achieved in a classroom of 30 students? Multiple intelligences and variations in temperaments and personality styles can be taken into account by implementing high and low structure times of the day or offering options for those who thrive in high structure and those who need low structure. Time to focus can be extended for the student who needs more, and redirection can be encouraged for the student who is energized to move on. Let's say a student needs or wants the whole day to work on something. Why is that bad? It is only a negative in the efficient, industrial, accountability model of learning (i.e., if you have a boss looking over your shoulder at your production for the day). But this is the opposite of how learning happens. (As it turns out, it is also the opposite of how adult humans work well, too!)

Approach Boredom and Discomfort

Just as failure has an important role to play in letting us become curious, so too does boredom. If necessity is the mother of invention, then boredom is the father of creativity. This is because out of the empty space emerges the unexpected. German philosopher Martin Heidegger shared the view that boredom can be transformative and creative. He wrote that boredom can take us out of clock time, away from its strict delineations, and entrance us instead with the wholeness of time, a "horizon . . . connected to what we call [a] moment of vision" (1995, p. 152).

One feature of our relationship with time is the tendency to fill every second. We are scared of silence, of dead space, of not filling every second of our lives with something. While waiting at the bus stop, we check our phones to see if anyone has called, check e-mail, or send text messages. We fill the time with our nervous energy. We are used to a fast paced, multitasking society; a culture of "speed, ease, constant activity, instant gratification, and sophisticated entertainment . . . [that has] lowered the tolerance of many of us for undesignated moments" (Belton, 2001, p. 817). We need to slow down ourselves. Our students and children have inherited that sense of urgency. Rushing has to do with an industrial, productivity model of education. But what if we imagined a more Zen model of the classroom? British education researcher Teresa Belton (2013) has discovered that the cultural expectation of constant activity is actually dulling the development of children's imaginations. Rather than filling every lull with activities and entertainment, lessons or screens, children need time to stand and stare. They need quiet and still time to think their own thoughts and to get to know their own intimate worlds. Boredom can be a highly creative state, opening up the development of internal stimulation. Instead of going for an external salve for boredom, just sitting with the discomfort can spur exploring the environment, developing an inner life, and having insights on a problem.

Like many college-level courses, in the seminars I teach, my students (many of whom are studying to be teachers) and I sit around a table together for three-hour blocks of time trying to question, dialogue, challenge, encourage, and excite one another. Over the years, I have noticed a funny phenomenon about the timeframe of the seminar. When conversation dries up, there are often very awkward and uncomfortable silences. As the facilitator, it is my job to guide us back to the text, draw out new questions, or make connections between the topics we are discussing. But if I jump in too quickly, there is a risk that my agenda begins to take priority. Often, I challenge myself to hang back and let a student take us someplace new. Everyone starts fidgeting, looking at the clock, hoping I will let them out early. It can be excruciating. But a few years ago, my students and I committed to hold the time of our class period together. With time being so precious, and opportunities for real deep dialogue being so few, we decided together that we were going to stay the entire class time, no matter what. A surprising thing happened. Once we were rid of the anxiety of trying to figure out when class would end, a new peaceful pace came over us. And lo and behold, new ideas, new insights, and deeper thinking began to emerge.

For writer Meera Syal, the solitude and lack of things to do during a childhood in a mining village opened up a life of spending time with elderly neighbors, observing and charting weather patterns, and most important, journaling. This freewheeling state builds on those things we do to just fill time. Likewise, for neuroscientist Susan Greenfield, being bored led to making up stories, drawing pictures, and spending hours at the local library (Belton, 2013). Research on imaginative storytelling in children shows a similar pattern: the most imaginative children draw upon their own direct experiences. Having experiences requires leaving open time for them to happen.

Struggling with boredom, and the transcendence of it, can be as powerful for learning as any challenge or complexity (Bruce, 1991). England's free school, the Summerhill School, includes allowing children to experience the full range of feelings associated with individual development, including boredom, stress, anger, disappointment, and failure, in its learning goals. A key part of their pedagogy is allowing boredom and impatience to happen and be transcended. Research on the effectiveness of their pedagogy has pointed to a complex, but integral, relationship between boredom and motivation, with boredom being understood as a "signal to change" (Goodsman, 1992, p. 177 cited in Belton & Priyadharshini, 2007). Similarly, research on motivation has shown that if children are encouraged to persevere on a task they initially find boring, their interest can become kindled via contemplation, daydreaming, and imagining alternatives (Darden, 1999; Dawley, 2006). Perhaps most important, when we fill the idle time with overstimulating experiences like TV or video games, we can rob children of the chance for inward activities, like observing, reflecting, and assimilating experience. We take away their chance to invent and develop their own pastimes—in essence we take away the building blocks of creativity and imagination (Belton, 2001; Belton & Priyadharshini, 2007).

Sometimes, when students are given a boring task, their curiosity has an opportunity to come out. They spontaneously embellish to make it more interesting for themselves. In one example, 5th graders intentionally increased the challenge of writing tasks in order to make it more interesting. Said one student, "If it said to write one sentence, I would write a lot more and make it more interesting" (Meyer & Turner, 2002, p. 109). In another example, 7th grade boys were working on a required science project to take care of live turtles. Once they started spending time with the turtles and each other, they decided to make the project more interesting by building ramps and holding races (Renninger & Hidi, 2002).

Curiosity Technique to Try: Loosen Up the Time Periods of the School Day

When I was in 5th grade, my teacher had surgery and was out for four weeks. A young, energetic substitute named Miss Proctor became our teacher. Miss Proctor irreverently threw aside the lesson book and spent the majority of every day reading children's fiction to us. We moved the desks out of the way and gathered around her as she read *The Secret Garden*, *A Wrinkle in Time*, *Anne of Green Gables*, and *From the Mixed-Up Files of Mrs. Basil E. Frankweiler*. I can still recall the exhilaration from not sticking to the schedule, and the feeling of letting all time stop to get lost in another world with bold Miss Proctor at the helm. Not only are those books still among my favorites, those four weeks are among the most memorable of my entire seven years in elementary school.

Teachers, if they are to construct a curiosity classroom, must be empowered to structure their days in a way that let the unexpected bubble up. Ideas of interest must be allowed to emerge. In the Reggio Emilia model, from the Italian city of the same name, the lesson plans are always subject to real-time revision using what is called *emergent curriculum*. In a Reggio Emilia classroom it is OK to throw the lesson plan out the window at any time—if a student notices something (a construction project across the street), if something current happens (a foot of snow falls), or if learning moments arise (conflict between friends). What could be more important or interesting than what the students are experiencing and feeling right here and right now? When time frames are too rigid, students compartmentalize: "School is boring, recess is fun" becomes their mantra. Once they have decided school is not their thing—or worse, a game that they play to please others—their curiosity has been squashed.

The Flow State

Can you remember a time when you were so immersed in a project that you didn't realize it had gotten dark and that you hadn't eaten in 12 hours? Historians claim that while he was painting the ceiling of the Sistine Chapel, Michelangelo worked for days at a time, not even stopping to rest or eat, until he would pass out from exhaustion, only to wake up refreshed and become completely immersed again. This extreme form of attention during movement is sometimes called flow and is often accompanied by clarity, confidence, a loss of the sense of time, serenity, and strong feelings of motivation and satisfaction. Across a wide variety of actions (for instance, visual arts, sports, music, or chess), the feeling of a flow state is associated with objective measures of high performance. Persons in a flow state may lose all awareness of other things, since all of their possible attention is focused, often effortlessly, on the task at hand (Csikszentmihalyi, 1997). To experience intense focus and effortlessness at the same time seems like a contradiction in terms, but this heightened, unforced concentration has a unique physiological pattern and seems to arise out of an interaction between positive affect and high attention (de Manzano, Theorell, Harmat, & Ullén, 2010).

When in a flow situation, worries, problems, and stress disappear for the simple reason that there is not enough attentional capacity for worries and also the actions at hand. According to ancient Japanese martial arts masters, a state of "no mind" (in which attention moves from one activity to another without the interference of thought) is the ideal. Indeed, when I am engrossed in complex physical actions like skiing or mountain biking, as soon as I pay attention to the moguls or rocks on the trail, I will fall. Instead, if I just let my attention flow, I become one with the mountain. As ancient Chinese poet Li Po so eloquently said, "We sit together, the mountain and me, until only the mountain remains."

How can teachers create that type of tremendous involvement, enjoyment, and excitement in school? Kindergarten teacher Leah Amaru has seen her kindergarten students enter a state of flow while developing critical literacy skills on "Fairytale Fridays." On these days, her students examine characters, settings, and plot lines and have very thoughtful discussions about ethical dilemmas. Then, the students do arts and craft projects corresponding with the fairytales. During one activity students were given various colors of construction paper and outlines of castles to color in and cut. The students were so engaged, so quietly and furiously working, that Ms. Amaru wiped everything else off of her agenda for the day and just went with it and let them continue. It took them all day, but they were so proud of their products. She commented, "When I first started teaching this day would have never happened! Many teachers feel there is so much to be packed into one day we often forget to step back and let the students take the lead of their learning. Although I pushed all of my other plans aside that day, I didn't have a panic attack!" (personal communication, June 26, 2015). These students spent time developing literacy skills (comprehension through critical literacy), fine motor skills (coloring, cutting, and pasting), math skills (shapes, symmetry, and spatial organization), planning, and oral language development. Coupling this with the intrinsic motivation of a flow state, it is difficult to think of a better use of their day.

Fostering a sense of flow in the classroom first requires changing our relationship to time. We must stop watching the clock and let how we feel guide how class periods are spent. Rather than having to switch topics during short blocks, children need to be able to become absorbed in their projects, their sports games, or their reading. We need to find a way to minimize distractions such as interruptions, changing goals arbitrarily, and the loudspeaker. William Ayers describes taking control over interruptions in his classroom as "creative insubordination" and says that such small subversions are the key to being an outstanding teacher. When the intercom interrupted his students for the seventh time one day, he brought out his screwdriver, took apart the speaker, clipped the wires, and reassembled the unit. He then sent a student to the office to let them know that the intercom was dysfunctional. It took them three years to repair it (Ayers, 2003, p. 29).

The reason that children report the best flow experience from extra-curricular activities like drama, orchestra, sports, or working on the student paper is because these activities often follow a more natural rhythm, rather than a jerky exposure to information (Csikszentmihalyi, 1997). How can we create that sense of flow? Removing clocks and deadlines may just be the answer. We need to think about learning in larger spans and considering wider perspectives. When infants first begin to eat solid foods, their parents often panic, because their eating may be sporadic. Pediatricians often tell parents of infants and toddlers not to worry. Instead of focusing on what the child has eaten in a single day, they need to be looking at the nutrition the child is getting over the course of a whole week. Could this also be true of learners? What if we had broader outcomes in mind over much larger swaths of time?

Free play is the epitome of the flow state (Csikszentmihalyi, 2000). Given the uninterrupted opportunity to go wherever their minds, bodies, hands, and brains take them, playing children control their own environments in unlimited experimental and imaginative ways. Results are irrelevant and time structures disappear. One homeschooling parent said that the flow state is very common for her children. They have gone into such deep engagement and attention while writing a graphic novel with a friend, creating a board game, making a stop-motion animation, creating a doll house from found materials, pro-gramming a computer game, and restoring a 1975 Camaro, to mention a few.

The biggest mistake we can make is to only allow play when "work" is finished. Education professor Susan Engel tells a story about a 5th grade science class she once observed in which students were doing a "hands-on" unit on the ancient Egyptians' use of wheels to transport the giant stones needed to build the pyramids. The children were given the step-by-step instructions guiding them toward the

Quick Recap

▶ Large and uninterrupted blocks of time allow curiosity to flourish.

▶ We have a tendency to disallow boredom and awkwardness, but it is important for students to learn how to transcend them.

▶ Idle time–like daydreaming, imagining, and doodling–actually supports curiosity.

▶ The flow state, by definition, cannot be rushed.

predetermined conclusion (the discovery that it was easier to pull the board if the dowels were used as wheels), which they were supposed to log on their worksheet. One group had abandoned the worksheet and the instructions for genuine, playful experimentation—they were intrigued by the equipment and were testing the multiple ways that the bar could be used with the spring scale attached. Without irony, their teacher Mrs. Parker called out to them, "OK, kids. Enough of that. I'll give you time to experiment at recess. This is time for science" (Engel, 2011, p. 625).

Curiosity Technique to Try: Rotate Longer Time Blocks into the Weekly Schedule

Often the structured time blocks are too short for the types of activities we want to do in our classes. Science labs have somehow earned a double period in order to complete their experiments, but what about literature classes? Or math classes? Some teachers have advocated for one subject per day. Others have begun to argue that we need to schedule in larger blocks that can be rotated so as to not privilege one academic discipline over another. According to one math teacher,

> The class I teach is 50 minutes long and we are always going overtime, much to the dismay of the teacher who uses the room after I do. We often don't hit our stride until 30 minutes in and I frequently have to interrupt activities in which the students are engrossed. I teach math as a hands-on activity and have had to interrupt such things as building a model of a four-dimensional tesseract out of rubber cement and Q-tips. Often times transferring an abstract concept to a concrete creation involves trial and error. Also, once a student has successfully completed something I like to ask them to think of another question to explore or find something else to try that would extend their understanding (e.g., "Is there a way to represent a tesseract in three dimensions?"). Having to stop at a predetermined time often shuts this process down in a way that is hard to restart at the beginning of the next class.

In Sum

Curiosity does not hold up under a rushed and impatient pace. Intense time constraints on our school days can limit meaningful engagement and discussion, ultimately hindering student development as learners. Teachers are often over-burdened by unrealistic expectations to cover massive amounts of content in short periods of time. The pressure to fill every second lessens the likelihood that unexpected and meaningful insights can arise. It is a grave mistake to prioritize content over intellectual hunger.

Instead, teachers want and deserve the time and freedom to determine how the day unfolds, even when that means scrapping the plan because an unexpected learning moment has emerged. Progressive education models like the Slow Schools Movement and the Montessori method empower students and teachers by letting them engage as long as they want to, which helps them approach and learn from unpredictable problems. If we want our students to be authentically curious, we must give them enough time to examine, ask, wonder, and discover.

7

Create Curiosity Habitats

The most effective kind of education is that a child should play amongst lovely things.

—Plato

To change classroom culture to curiosity mode, we must not only shift habits, we must also shift habitats. Not surprisingly, the physical environment where learning happens is a powerful determinant in fostering and maintaining curiosity. Creating a habitat that nourishes curiosity requires that every now and then we look around our classrooms with fresh eyes and reexamine the messages implicit in the space. In what ways does this classroom setup support originality and discovery? Are there varied spaces in which students can inhabit different frames of mind, such as out of the way places where students can work quietly and calmly, and focus for long periods of time? Are there spots that invite students to work together or corners that can be transformed for a particular project? Is there an available supply of open-ended materials? Are there places of varied perspectives and varied brightness? If children were to enter the space, would they feel a sense of communion and ownership? (Curtis & Carter, 2015). Carefully setting up classroom environments gives us an opportunity to connect children to a sense of place—the people, places, and natural world around them—and foster their growing minds.

Just like the air we breathe, the design of the physical environments we spend time in is often invisible to us (Zane, 2015). But classroom spaces affect how we think, feel, and behave in myriad ways. Every environment communicates values or beliefs about the people who use the space, and the activities that take place there (Curtis & Carter, 2015). Spaces can demand creativity and ingenuity, responsibility and compassion, or passivity and compliance (Hetland, Winner, Veenema, & Sheridan, 2007). Since children spend about 1,300 hours per year in a school building (Day, 1995), many pedagogues now believe that classroom spaces can affect students as much as their parents and teachers do. That is why the classroom environment is sometimes referred to as "the third teacher" (Strong-Wilson & Ellis, 2007, p. 40).

The Learning Environment's Affordances

We design our world, while our world acts back on us, and designs us.

—Anne-Marie Willis, "Ontological Designing"
in *Design Philosophy Papers Collection*

In the 1950s, perceptual psychologist James Gibson began to study vision—in particular, how the photoreceptors in the retina of the eye translate patterned light into the knowledge and understanding we immediately feel when we encounter objects and actions. He coined the term "affordances" to capture those things that the environment gives to the perceptual relationship, launching the field of ecological psychology (Gibson, 1950). From this research, we now know that we need to take into account what the environment offers to the learner, because values and meanings can be directly perceived within its composition and layout.

The affordances of a physical space are critical when it comes to inspiring curiosity. Consider for a minute, in what ways can emptiness or blank spaces allow ideas and innovations, curiosity and questions to bubble up? How can interesting places to land one's eyes and the inspiration of others' work allow innovation to the surface? Since curiosity is an essential element of child learning and development, we need to shift schools completely away from a "cells and bells" model of design and start to consider what our ideal learning environment might look like. Would it be open and collaborative as a hacker space, or small and snug as a cubby? We may start to wonder, how much stuff should be in the room? How should areas of the room be arranged, and what would they afford? What should decorate the walls? How flexible could the space be? Who owns it? What specifically should the curiosity classroom afford?

When used well, spaces can guide learners toward deep and meaningful engagement. Students quickly come to feel what a space has to offer them and internalize its messages. For example, seating students at individual desks rather than grouping them at tables supports the belief that children learn best through individual work. Grouping students according to ranking on a test conveys narratives about hierarchy and power. If you believe that children benefit from handling their own conflicts, then you will want to provide ways for them to encounter those opportunities, encouraging negotiating by placing benches rather than chairs at the tables (Curtis & Carter, 2015).

When you design a curiosity classroom, you send a message of respect and appreciation for those who inhabit and use the space (Bunting, 2004). Even classroom shelves, when mindfully arranged, can be transformed into a living archive of the learning that happened in that space, like a collection of rocks from a nature walk, a half-finished puzzle, or a project waiting to be taken on (Strong-Wilson & Ellis, 2007). Storage can be raised to an art form when you use unusual and thought-provoking textures to display possibility, like scissors kept in the holes of bricks, paint brushes standing within a bowl of corn kernels in an early childhood classroom, or rainbow color-coded books in a high school English class. Organizing spaces is an act of making them beautiful. Children can think creatively about how and where to display their schoolwork and treasures in unique ways when you offer many surfaces, such as walls, floors, windows and shelves (Deviny, Duncan, Harris, Rody, & Rosenberry, 2010).

In the Reggio Emilia model of education, virtually every classroom display comes from the work of the students. Displays are used to tell an authentic story of the learning experiences behind them. When children embark on a project, their teachers carefully document the stages of learning through-out the process. This is then represented and installed for the community, as a living testimony to what happened within the shared learning space. Multiple stories can be woven together via students' portfolios, photos, videos, documentation panels, drawings, three-dimensional structures, or written words (Strong-Wilson & Ellis, 2007). Such documentation captures projects for posterity, while also reflecting the history of the relationship between the people, environment, and pedagogy. After completing a particularly challeng-ing project, you may want to give your students an opportunity to showcase their work by turning your classroom into a public gallery, and then invite the public to come in and look. At Walnut Hill School in Natick, Massachusetts, one teacher prefers to exhibit student work in various stages of completion, rather than just showing finished products (Hetland et al., 2007). This lets the entire community know that the value of the learning journey is equally important to the outcome.

In classroom design, as in architecture, form should follow function. When you set up your classroom you are not merely communicating your own priorities, but you are making clear the foundational beliefs on which your entire school or program is built. At the Boston Arts Academy, teachers Kathleen, Beth, and Mickey have deliberately designed their walls to reflect the values of the school. Hanging among student artwork, visitors will find goals, instructions for routines, and inspiring quotes (Hetland et al., 2007). If you and your colleagues believe that activities should be open-ended, as Dewey espoused, then you will have materials handy to be used in creative ways and you will have furniture that can be moved to accommodate spontaneous changes in configuration. If you are at a Montessori-based school, classroom configurations should be carefully chosen, with few colors and posters on the walls. The learning materials you provide should be made from all natural resources, rather than synthetic ones, creating a calming environment. If your program resonates with Rudolf Steiner's ideas of harmony with nature, you will offer timeless, handcrafted manipulatives and furniture with muted colors (Curtis & Carter, 2015).

Exciting spaces lead to increased exploration and critical thinking. To foster problem solving, inquiry, and serious focused work, areas should include more angular furniture, with sturdy, supportive chairs. For collaboration, which asks students to let their guards down and connect, the space requires more comfortable seating arrangements and moveable stations. Just using a variety of types of chairs can naturally add interest and expanded relationship opportunities (Zane, 2015). Let your classroom space speak to the learners and invite them to be curious. For instance, place small mirrors in unique places around the classroom, prisms next to sunlight, or blank pieces of paper with questions to respond to. Provoke surprise, and welcome your students to get engaged, respond to their environments, and see them in new and unexpected ways (Strong-Wilson & Ellis, 2007). In all shared spaces, once creativity and energy are sparked, they multiply. As urban studies activist and writer Jane Jacobs has said, "Life attracts life" (1961, p. 349).

On the other hand, corners crowded with stuff and cluttered walls, shelves, and countertops can create a feeling of chaos. Since children are extra-sensitive to aesthetic information, jumbled, messy spaces are distracting and make learning more difficult. In her insightful piece "Consider the Walls," early childhood education professor Patricia Tarr put herself in the shoes of a young child immersed in the environment of an over-decorated classroom, and wondered how the visual busy-ness could impact the child's concentration:

> From a small chair in a corner, I counted 19 different, decorated, scalloped borders segmenting portions of the bulletin boards lining the walls. The boards were filled with words: a word wall, class rules, a calendar, alphabets, numbers, shapes and colors, and a plethora of cartoon people and animals, each with a message and at least 50 of them

with horseshoe-shaped smiles rather like a capital *U*. ... St. Patrick's Day mobiles created from brightly painted rainbows and black-line masters hung from the ceiling just above the children's heads. Rainbows, leprechauns, and pots of gold jiggled before my eyes. (Tarr, 2004, p. 88)

Tarr wondered about the implicit messages being transmitted by these displays, and hypothesized that their canned or stereotyped messages likely silence children from expressing their more authentic, lived learning experiences.

Quick Recap

▶ Curiosity thrives in certain places and spaces.

▶ Arranging the space can be a powerful factor for achieving instructional goals.

▶ To create a curiosity classroom, we need to shift away from the "cells and bells" model of school.

Curiosity Technique to Try: Become Aware of Space

Part of setting up a curiosity classroom is deciding the particular values you want to convey through your learning environment. To begin this process, go on a classroom tour either in real life (in your school building) or on the Internet. Try to find as many diverse examples of using the space as you can. For instance, survey the classrooms of different grade levels, different cultures, and different types of buildings. For each image or space you enter, ask yourself these questions: If space could speak, what would each classroom tell you? If you had to imagine a phrase—a motto—that would capture this classroom, what would it be? Imagine yourself at the age of the students who use this space. In the students' voice, write four sentences that would come from their perspective on this space, having first entered. (Finish this sentence for your imaginary student. "This classroom is _____ because of _____.") Name the dominant colors, sounds, and sources of light, smells, and temperatures of the room. Seating design can be territorial (space arranged by individual desk ownership) or functional (space arranged by a specific activity). There may be an "action zone" where increased involvement between teachers and students occurs (Higgins, Hall, Wall, Woolner, & McCaughey, 2005). What would you call this part of the classroom? Once you are aware of the role of space as "the third teacher" you can make decisions that open up your space for curiosity. This can be a wonderfully revealing exercise to do with colleagues, and a creative tool for professional development.

Active and Dynamic

Curiosity is active. We humans have developed and evolved our complex brains within a dynamic surround. In fact, for 99 percent of the time that humans have lived on earth, we have spent our days outside hunting for or gathering food, avoiding predators, and moving from place to place. Back then we needed to pay attention to survive. Consequently, our brains have been set up to operate best in changing environments (Gray, 2013; Medina, 2014). Indeed, children devote most of their waking hours to movement. Running, jumping, rolling and playing, doing somersaults, and wrestling are what it means to be a kid. Children's bodies, metabolisms, and bone structure are designed to be active all day long (Imus, 2008). Rather than trying to get children to sit still and stop fidgeting, we must design learning spaces that embrace children's movement and action as necessary prerequisites for developing attention (Ostroff, 2014).

Dynamic and changeable spaces afford curiosity. Too often once a room arrangement has been put into place, it rarely changes. Some teachers tend to teach according to the configuration already in the room, using table sizes to decide group sizes, for example, rather than making careful pedagogical decisions (McNamara & Waugh, 1993). On the other hand, one recent research study found that teachers who modified and changed their classrooms regularly to create better, more effective learning spaces were also more likely to use innovative pedagogies and to collaborate with their colleagues (Bissell, 2004). Similarly, students who are encouraged to take things from one area to another in the classroom, or to play with materials in unexpected ways, show more complex problem-solving skills and more creative thinking. Configurations of furniture greatly impact how learning occurs. Beth, an art teacher, sets up the studio in a completely different arrangement when she begins a unit on clay than she does when she starts a painting unit. She accommodates different vantage points, social groupings, and uses of materials (Hetland et al., 2007). Other art teachers, like Jim, avoid determining the space before the students enter. He lets students grab a stool and pick a vantage point to learn—encouraging them to try several spots before settling on where to draw. When we want to shake things up, we need a space that can afford changing locations, exploring new surroundings with bodies and minds.

When we design a space for curiosity, we should be mindful of how the space allows for varying paces throughout the day. When we want to slow the pace, we can create alcoves and place furniture in hallways to discourage that high-speed traffic and create places of pause. We can create cozy retreats and spots to hang out. Students should feel that they belong to the learning space and that the space belongs to them. They should be free to go from a vast openness into a small secure corner if need be.

Humans flourish in environments that allow many potential postures. Professional workspaces that value curiosity and creativity are now setting up areas that allow their employees to lie on the floor, perch on the back of a couch, bounce on an exercise ball, pace around the room, or even do some chin-ups on exposed beams—all during "work" sessions. Being able to move supports being able to think, especially creative and divergent thinking. Standing work stations are the rage not just because they afford better posture, but because they also promote more innovative thinking. We need to mix up our bodies' orientations in order to think in varying styles. My husband, Rob, realized this when he got his first standing workstation. If he was coming up with ideas or brainstorming with colleagues, standing was the best position. But when he needed to think more analytically, for example, when writing code for computer programming, sitting down was the posture that worked best. You, too, can find ways for your students to move their bodies in your classroom, such as leaving space free, setting up nonprescriptive seating, and offering places to work with multiple seating heights (Doorley & Witthoft, 2012).

Think about nonobvious ways to make your classroom space dynamic. Children might slip off their shoes as they walk into the classroom, as a physical reminder that they are changing states and entering learning mode. Martina Delancy, a New York photographer who specializes in working with young children, has stumbled upon a technique to calm her agitated subjects and get them to relax in front of the camera. Moving children from one state to another is a key of her success at capturing them in images. She built a wooden cube with one open side, no larger than 2.5 square feet, and covered it with soft white fur. Upset children often feel safe and cozy in that space, almost like infants being swaddled. When the families come in to shoot the photos, they are amazed at how relaxed their young children feel and behave (and how genuinely they smile) within such a tiny space.

Professor and Dialogue Center director Margaret Anderson radically altered her physical classroom space as an entrée to get her students to open up and discuss difficult topics such as racism, sexism, and cultural violence. Confronting their own individual prejudices and those of the surrounding culture was very difficult for students. Anderson realized that she really wanted them to be in a completely different mode, to crack open those views that have been formed and hardened and to let their guards down. Instead of chairs and desks, Anderson's dialogue space is now filled with oversize beanbags in which three or more students nestle together. Seminaring in beanbag chairs changed the students' classroom presence in profound and transformative ways:

> Since the beanbags afford an immediate transformation of where you are, *who you are, who's in charge, and who's in power* all shift. When you are sitting in beanbags, you can't have that standard response that you've had delivered to you. Taboo topics typically make people tense up and feel uncomfortable, or repeat back opinions and responses that they have heard from others in predictable ways. But in the Dialogue Center beanbag chairs, students are in an entirely different state of mind. The classroom space is such a different context that it almost jolts or re-energizes them. It is an invitation; a dare. In a weird way, the students get released from all that self-consciousness, just like little kids getting comfy. Sometimes they close their eyes and lean back—then get inspired and pipe up thoughtfully. Their bodies and their thoughts are loosening. They are sitting next to people—getting comfortable physically, which facilitates getting comfortable with uncomfortable ideas. The space forces a juxtaposition of opposing postures—being flexible and loose, but willing to hold differing perspectives. The beanbag chairs keep the students open, instead of them closing up. (Margaret Anderson, personal communication, September 23, 2015)

In middle and high schools in San Francisco, redesigning the cafeterias into student-centered and dynamic spaces has completely revolutionized the way kids eat, and in turn, how ready they are to learn. Like many large, urban school districts, more than half of the students in the San Francisco Unified School District qualify for reduced or free lunch. But what has baffled administrators and teachers for decades is the fact that only a small percentage of the students eat lunch regularly. We all know how important healthy foods are for brain function and cognition. San Francisco educators turned to the design firm IDEO to help solve their problem, which turned out to be an issue of stagnant space (Stinson, 2014).

The designers at IDEO began by asking the students what was important to them, something that had never been done. Younger children were just coming in from recess when they ate lunch. Assembly line, inefficiency, and one-size-fits-all models (where ambiance and environment are sacrificed to save money) are the opposite of dynamic, and actually cost money in the long run on wasted food and undernourished, frustrated students. They replaced that mentality with student-centered design: The cafeteria was outfitted with soft lighting and ambient music, and the students were invited to sit at round tables and eat family style rather than spending most of that down time in a line. Peers now take turns serving their friends' meals family style, beginning with vegetables. When students finish that course, they are served more food that comes around on carts. The moving sequence encourages children to eat what they have first, and finish what is on their plates. Each child gets a turn being table captain. Minor tweaks like removing food from packaging and putting it in a bowl made significant changes in the amount of food that the kids would eat. One of the designers recalled, "We served exact same food the cafeteria served, and all of the students said, 'This isn't the same food'" (Stinson, 2014).

Like all of us, students want a space that they have some ownership and power over. IDEO let them design it—from the cafeteria artwork to the seating. The middle school children wanted a cafeteria that was more than just

Quick Recap

- ▶ Our environments are filled with rich, textured, meaningful information for perception called affordances.
- ▶ Settings afford particular responses to them.
- ▶ Curiosity is an active process. Curiosity spaces should be dynamic and embrace movement.
- ▶ School spaces should accommodate varied paces, postures, configurations, and displays.

a place to eat. They wanted an activity hub where they could hang out with friends on couches, read a book, or do homework. IDEO designed a system where kids could grab a pre-made meal from a vending machine or mobile cart and enjoy it outside in a lounge area. High school students wanted even more mobility. They asked to be able to leave campus and get food elsewhere at times, so IDEO created an RSVP system where students could check in to let the kitchen know whether or not they would be eating in the cafeteria, and they could also pre-order what they would like and rate the quality of what they just ate. Empowering them was a significant part of the design (Stinson, 2014).

One of the first goals in fostering curiosity and ownership is to equalize the respective status of students and teachers. When you walk into a curiosity classroom, it may be difficult to tell who's teaching and who's learning. Innovation thrives on this kind of equality. When a boss or a teacher is standing at the head of the room, students become more reluctant to share their ideas. "What if the boss doesn't like it?" may always be in the back of their minds. Reconfiguring the physical relationship is a powerful signal that participation is truly welcome. The result is that you get better ideas out in the open, where they can grow (Doorley & Witthoft, 2012). Begin to deliberately alter your classroom environment and you will reveal what enhances ideas and collaboration and what doesn't, what boosts creativity and what doesn't.

Curiosity Technique to Try: Let Your Students Set Up the Classroom

In the children's book *A World of Your Own*, author Laura Carlin asks children, "If you were creating a world of your own, what would it look like?" and then invites them to look, draw, and make a world of their own imaginations, beginning with what they see, and then, using her prompts and questions, opening up the world to infinite possibilities (e.g., "Would you build your house out of brick or out of jelly? Would it be on the ground or in a tree? Would your shops sell envelopes and sweets or shoes for superheroes? Would you ride a train to town or a dinosaur?").

Although we may be more grounded by physics and funds, we should nevertheless open up possibilities for kids by letting them imagine and design their own spaces. If we want our students to be mindful of the effect that space has upon their work, and we want them to take ownership of their learning, we should give them a chance to take responsibility for setting up the environments that support their work. Involving users in the design of teaching and learning spaces benefits students and teachers alike. It encourages active citizenship, rather than the passive receipt of education, and is a terrific opportunity to reengage students with learning (McGregor, 2004).

Begin by doing less, even though your impulse might be to take care of every detail of setting up your space. Open space provides a buffer for identifying, absorbing, and responding to unanticipated needs. Use modular and movable furniture and displays so that physical change is easy (Doorley & Witthoft, 2012). You may want to leave a corner or an area of your classroom open, and structure in the design of that space as a part of the lesson. Let's say that your students are making plaster maps of their chosen countries for a geography lesson or solving problems together for a math relay. In preparation for the project, like a pre-lab in the physical sciences, build classroom design into the preparation and planning stage of the assignment. This encourages carefully thinking about process, as well as metacognition. In teams, have students create proposals for the setup of the space that will work best and present those proposals to the group (small whiteboards are great tools for mock-ups of a layout of the furniture, for instance). The group can vote and decide which design model to use. After the assignment is complete, the students can critique what worked and did not work in terms of their designs. Would it have been better for them to work on their maps on the floor? Would small tables have worked better? Would collaboration have been easier if all of the students were at one big table? The classroom suddenly transforms itself into a hacker space or a workshop, affording excitement for the next hands-on project. If we set the expectation that each person is a steward of the space, he or she will come to care for it. At the same time, if it's not working, students will feel empowered to change things up (Doorley & Witthoft, 2012). As a classroom gets used in new ways, new needs emerge. Leave room to adapt. Creative people regularly generate surprising ideas, and all kids are creative people. The space needs to morph to support, organize, and display unpredictable ideas and creations.

Bright, Loud, Dim, Quiet

The learning environment awakens curiosity by not being overstimulating. Learners absorb everything through their senses. Too much color, sound, or busyness can take children away from the depth and focus that nurtures creativity and wonder. On the other hand, there are times when the classroom space needs to be energized and electrified, to propel curiosity onward.

The curiosity classroom should be mindful of acoustics—good for speech and hearing, as the auditory can both energize and calm students. A host of research has shown that young learners are more profoundly affected by noise than adults, across speech perception, listening comprehension, memory, reading, and writing tasks (Klatte, Bergstroem, & Lachmann, 2013). At the same time, we now know that music positively affects students' learning and engagement by establishing attention, creating desired atmospheres, enhancing imagination, building anticipation, improving memory, and releasing tension (Brewer, 1995). Teachers at the Boston Arts Academy sometimes hold open studio periods, when students are free to drop in and work on ongoing projects. These time periods are filled with a social buzz, and they are best paired with popular, loud music. Jim often puts on upbeat music in the afternoons, when students need an energy boost. For projects that require quiet and calm concentration, complex jazz pieces can softly support focus and decision making (Hetland et al., 2007).

One way that teachers can use music to help students engage with and remember learning experiences is by creating a soundtrack for a learning activity. The soundtrack increases mental, physical, and emotional interest. When information is put to rhythm and rhyme these musical elements will provide a hook for recall. For example, in her social studies class, Chris Brewer reads quotes from Chief Joseph and a brief overview of his tribe's famous journey toward Canada, while playing native music in the background. This introduction to the "Last Free Days of the Nez Perce" is emotionally powerful and more memorable because the music allows students' moods to be transformed into the mood of the scene. When teaching her students about the flow of electrons, Brewer puts on Ray Lynch's "Celestial Soda Pop" and asks her students to physically role-play flowing electricity, with some students behaving as stationary neutrons and protons and others as moving electrons. Then, when they add "free electrons" (like a battery would), out comes an electrical current! Ray Lynch's upbeat song keeps the students moving and makes the imaginary scenario both more real and more fun (Brewer, 1995).

Similar to sound, children are extremely sensitive and responsive to nuances in lighting and color. The curiosity classroom should have good lighting and, whenever possible, natural light. In the 1970s, school architects made the shortsighted decision to design classrooms with either small or no windows as a means of removing visual distractions and helping kids focus on their work. But for most of us, spaces without visual connections to the outside create a closed-in feeling and increase anxiety. Kids in schools that feel like prisons focus less on learning and more on escape. In addition, we now know that natural light is important for learning. Our brains have evolved in those conditions. Whereas artificial light is a long light wave, the body's circadian rhythm system (which governs its waking and sleeping patterns) responds to shorter waves, which suppress the natural hormone melatonin, stimulating alertness via the hormone serotonin (Falchi, Cinzano, Elvidge, Keith, & Haim, 2011).

Almost a half century later, architects are espousing the exact opposite, and the results speak for themselves. Rather than distracting students, natural light actually helps students focus (Fielding, 2006). In a recent series of studies involving 20,000 students in California, Colorado, and Massachusetts, students' standardized test scores increased by 26 percent when primarily natural lighting illuminated their classrooms, compared with those who relied mainly on artificial light (Hershong Mahone Group, 2003).

In another recent study, people who work in offices without windows were compared to those who have windows. The results showed that those with windows slept almost a full hour more per night. They also showed higher sleep quality and fewer sleep disturbances. They also had fewer physical problems and reported a significantly higher vitality and quality of life (Boubekri, Cheung, Reid, Wang, & Zee, 2014). "The extent to which daylight exposure impacts office workers is remarkable. Day-shift office workers' quality of life and sleep may be improved via emphasis on light exposure and lighting levels in current offices as well as in the design of future offices," said study coauthor Ivy Cheung, a neuroscience doctoral candidate at Northwestern University. Imagine how this affects children.

Uniform lighting is another rule that architects of learning spaces are beginning to rethink. Outmoded school building specifications and codes tend to call for uniform brightness, which is good for assembly lines, but more recent research in the field of perception has indicated that a fuller spectrum of light, more like that of natural daylight, makes for a happier, healthier learning space (Fielding, 2006). Some teachers, like Jim, an art teacher who works at the Walnut Hill School in Massachusetts, change the lighting for particular assignments and lessons, even during a single class. Jim may pull the shades or use a spotlight or line the window shades with small white lights. This greatly affects the mood of the room and brings out different attitudes and perceptions (Hetland et al., 2007). English teacher Sana Fazal has found that lowering the lighting encourages her students to open up more in discussions of complex literature. It almost creates an intimate, café-like setting where high school students feel that they can switch into a gentler and more intellectually playful style of thinking. Almost like the hidden cave in which students in the film *The Dead Poets Society* meet, merely softening the glare softens Fazal's students' inhibitions. There is no reason why teachers in other disciplines cannot also use light to influence learning.

The quality of the physical environment directly influences student learning and achievement (Earthman, 2004). At the School of the Built Environment at the University of Salford professor Peter Barrett and

Quick Recap

▶ Curiosity thrives during creative collaboration–spaces should be set up for varied groupings of students.

▶ Physical space can be reconfigured to break traditional hierarchies like the "sage on the stage" mentality.

▶ Learning environments should not overstimulate the senses.

▶ Music can create diverse atmospheres and is a wonderful tool for curiosity.

▶ Good lighting, especially natural light, is best for both human functioning and learning.

his colleagues recently examined the impact of the spaces for learning in seven schools on more than 750 primary students' reading, writing, and math progression over the course of the academic year. Students' engagement and learning progress were most affected by the color of the room, the flexibility of the space, the complexity of the environment, and the lighting (Barrett, Zhang, Moffat, & Kobbacy, 2013).

Curiosity Technique to Try: Mix Up the Modalities

When you are designing particular lessons, imagine the physical and visceral space that would make it work best. For instance, 3rd grade teacher Enrique Floria introduces fractions by teaching his students to fold origami. When it comes time for the folding, he gathers the desks around in a tight circle and whispers the instructions. Something about the quiet in the room lets students know that this is a gentle activity that requires great care. Moving their bodies slowly and deliberately is the path to a successful crane or owl. What about whispered discussions of high school philosophy in the hallway? Or co-outlining first drafts of an essay within small circles of movable cubes around standing whiteboards in the four corners, based on your interest area?

Just as Japanese tea ceremonies happen in cozy, quiet spaces, and little spots, sometimes it's best to turn the music loud and clear everything out in order to get ideas going for creative response. Is there a particular song that you can play to let your class know that it's time to cut loose and be silly or time to be still? History as role-play, for example, can involve creating the atmosphere that was felt at the time. Does the room need to be sparse or ominous? Benign violations can make a space playful, and as we know, play is the best way for children to learn (McGraw & Warren, 2010). Forts and tents made from pillows are not just for little ones—once the space has been made playful, the role-playing will naturally follow.

Curiosity Technique to Try: Conduct Lessons Outside

In the curiosity classroom, we must celebrate the old adage of the Norwegians, "There is no such thing as bad weather, just bad clothing." We do not need to reserve outside time for recess, breaks, or perfect spring afternoons. We also do not need to reserve our outdoor time for lessons that can only be done outside, like nature walks or observations. Try bringing your class out in the light for a lesson that could be just as easily done anywhere. If you are doing a math lesson on shapes, have the students make themselves into a giant square, then circle, then oval. How long does it take for them to reconfigure into perfect formation? Play some music and students can march into new formations, marching band style. For learning about comparing fractions, divide students into groups and then remove 1/3 versus 1/4 of the students. Can they viscerally get the picture?

Children are intrigued by natural phenomena and the world around them, and being outdoors provides the types of sensory stimulation that our nervous systems have evolved within—light, color, sound, reflection, and motion. They need opportunities to observe closely and take action to test out their theories of how the world works—whether to stop, look up, and listen when a bird goes by, or whether to document the tiny ecosystem functioning within a patch of the play yard grass (Curtis & Carter, 2015).

Read poetry or stories under a tree. Have students read to their reading buddies on benches. Write stories together in different corners of the playground. If it is cold out, wear warm coats and sing songs while walking. If you are lucky enough to teach at a school with grounds and yards, use them as teachable space, rather than feeling stuck inside the classroom.

We can blame the fact that our schools have become "fortresses" on the lower engagement from students, teachers, parents, and community members (Horne, 2004). Education innovators challenge us teachers to "tear down the school walls."

In Sum

In order to cultivate curiosity, classroom spaces should be learner centered. Our brains have evolved to thrive in moving and changing environments. Therefore, varying paces and postures, as well as lighting and sound, can allow curiosity to bubble up. If we create classroom habitats that mirror our complexity as learners, we may find that one-size-fits-all classroom spaces will disappear, replaced by student-owned learning labs and curiosity exploration centers (Stevenson, 2007). The end goal is to create a space that affords curiosity by virtue of being unique. When a place feels special to the students, it has a cascading impact. Beyond just being an enjoyable place to be, students take pride in their shared space. With pride comes sense of ownership, with ownership belonging (Doorley & Witthoft, 2012).

Conclusion

Prioritize Processes of Learning

*I think you should learn, of course, and some days
you must learn a great deal. But you should also
have days when you allow what is already in you to
swell up inside of you until it touches everything.*

*—From the Mixed-Up Files of
Mrs. Basil E. Frankweiler*

In an ancient and sacred ritual, Buddhist monks spend days or even
weeks painstakingly laying hundreds of millions of grains of colored
sand in a circular design called a mandala, which includes geometric
shapes and spiritual icons. Mandalas are usually several feet wide
and take up to 30 hours to create. The monks working on them have
to perfect a particular type of light breathing so that the grains of
sand do not move from their breath. Mandalas are thought to heal
both those who work on them and those who witness the meticulous
process of constructing them. The monks work from the inside out,

using tiny metal funnels, because the colors and patterns so easily smudge. When the mandala is finally complete, blessings are offered, and then the mandala is quickly and quietly destroyed. For the monks, the process of creating the mandala is sacred in and of itself, and the end product matters not.

Focusing on Skills Rather Than Content

Children must be taught what to think, not how to think.

—Margaret Mead

In a way, building a curiosity classroom is like building a sand mandala in that the goal of the curiosity classroom is not necessarily finding but exploring (Shonstrom, 2014). When students gain the tools to follow their curiosity, then the end product is somewhat irrelevant, since they can learn any content throughout their lives. Indeed, more recent definitions of learning in the field of cognitive science acknowledge that it is a process first and foremost, since it may not be accompanied by any measureable product (Lachman, 1997). As the old saying goes, "Give a man a fish and you feed him for a day. Teach a man to fish and you feed him for a lifetime" (Ritchie, 1885/2008).

The triumph of curiosity for learning is celebrated in the Dr. Seuss storybook *Hooray for Diffendoofer Day*. At the Diffendoofer School, the teachers make up their own rules—like the librarian who tells the students to be louder in the library, the music teacher who makes bagpipes out of straws and socks, or the art teacher who paints pictures hanging from his knees. Until standardized testing comes along. And if the students and teachers of Diffendoofer don't pass the test, the school will be torn down, forcing all of them to go to school in dreary Flobbertown! But in a shocking twist, they ace the test. Despite questions about things they had "never seen or heard . . . somehow answered them, enjoying every word." How did they do it? Beloved Miss Bonkers says it best, "You've learned the things you need to pass that test and many more . . . We've taught you that the earth is round, that red and white make pink. And something else that matters more—We've taught you how to think" (Seuss, Prelutsky, & Smith, 1998).

One reason that content should not be the priority is that content is transient. Students of all ages who do well in a course or lesson often proceed to quite quickly forget what they have "learned." How much do you remember from the foreign language courses you took in high school? Unless you had concrete experiences using those words and grammatical configurations, it is likely that you remember very little. (It is actually a blessing that we remember little of these details—our brains are efficient process-oriented organs that do not allow factoids to take up space. They quickly prune things that are not useful and being used in real time.) It is true, almost all of the stuff we have been required to remember in school is forgotten. Facts, dates, and definitions are lost within months, days, or even hours if we don't use them in meaningful ways. We all know this, yet the technique of schooling continues to consist of stuffing facts into students' short-term memories (Kohn, 2011).

We are bad at remembering facts. Even the best students do not remember the details from material they have mastered and aced tests on if they are not used. It is now well established that students retain little if any concrete knowledge from the content of their K–12 education (Barrows et al., 1981; Bauerlein, 2008; National Commission on Excellence in Education, 1983). This is because our sensory and attention systems are very selective about the information they take in. If we really perceived and paid attention to every detail of every object in our surround (the hum of the computer and the heat coming on and the temperature of the room and the dancing light on the wall and the siren in the distance) we would be overwhelmed by the deluge and unable to do what we need to do. By filtering what we take in, we are selecting what is important.

In a now famous study, researchers asked Harvard University students the simple question at commencement "Why does the earth have seasons?" and discovered that nearly everyone answered incorrectly. It was not that these students hadn't learned that the tilt of the earth's axis causes seasons; most had probably learned that in the elementary school. It was simply that the information held no relevance or immediacy; they had done no cognitive manipulation—no real thinking about it or acting upon it—to make it stick in their memories (Schneps, 1989). Another study showed that college students who majored in marketing were no more successful in marketing in the long term than those who majored in something else. Most knowledge about consumer behavior was forgotten soon after the students completed their Consumer Marketing course (Hunt, Chonko, & Wood, 1986). Says Erik Shonstrom (2014),

> I was once a math and science teacher at a crowded urban middle school in Los Angeles. I exhausted myself trying to teach students a modicum of skills. Like other teachers, I put in obscenely long days working predominantly with students from poor neighborhoods, trying to impart a basic understanding of the math and science principles the kids would need for any shot at college-track classes in high school. What I didn't do was expose math and science for what they are— two of the last great frontiers for the insatiably curious, realms where imagination and dreams can intuit whole new worlds, places where wondering—wonderment—is the only tool you really need.

Even students who figure out a clever way to remember the facts and tidbits they were taught cannot necessarily make connections among them or apply them in any meaningful way to real-life problems. As educational philosopher and critic Alfie Kohn has said, "Just knowing a lot of facts doesn't mean you're smart" (Kohn, 2011, p. 2). In other words, factual material rarely corresponds to deep understanding. Although some content is important (e.g., it may be useful in life to memorize the multiplication tables or the state capitals), we must remember that the human brain is less detail oriented and more process oriented. Students remember actions and things they manipulate, interact with, and do. But more than anything, students remember things that have importance for them. The memory systems of the brain are summarizers and meaning-makers, not video recorders or fact repositories. If the teacher shows us how to bake corn bread to learn about the conditions of the Underground Railroad or to create a skit about the Spanish Civil War, we will mostly remember what we spent our time engaged with (e.g., baking

Quick Recap

▶ The process of learning is infinitely more important than the product of learning.

▶ The human brain is process oriented.

▶ Almost all of the content we have been required to learn in school is forgotten.

▶ Those things that students learn deeply and remember have relevance and meaning to them.

▶ Student must think about or act upon ideas to retain them.

▶ Creating the curiosity classroom involves letting go of control and trusting that learning will happen.

the bread and making up the skit). In this way, what we really learn (and remember) from our schooling are those experiences that had meaning for us (Willingham, 2009). By imbuing what we experience with meaning, we can trim down those facts and data points that are less useful and find a sense of coherence in the world. Our memories are created and recreated in social interactions in which we share our stories with others (Fivush, 2008). When we remember something, be it about our first kiss or cell division or *The Catcher in the Rye,* our brains spin the tale a bit differently each time (more coherent, more focused, more entertaining). We quickly forget isolated bits of information that we have never mixed with meaning (dates of wars, symbols from the periodic table).

Music students can get the chords and notes correct but never develop their own interpretation of the feeling of a piece of music. Math students can memorize theorems, but unless they become mathematical in their thinking, they will not solve any new problems. We can test foreign language students on the number of words they have memorized, but this corresponds little to being able to understand or speak the language fluently. History exams ask for dates and facts, but historians search for nuanced narratives and know full well that one story could never come to capture the lessons and experiences of the past.

Focusing on the Journey Rather than the Outcome

Learning is not a linear process with inputs and outputs that can be easily measured. We have used industrial methods to design our schools, and out of tradition, have come to believe that an input-output, linear model is how learning will occur best. But that is not how our brains have evolved. We have evolved hunting and gathering in cycles. We have seasons of great energy and seasons of rest. We are constantly moving and adapting to changing conditions (Gray, 2013). To prepare the ground for the curiosity classroom, we must first trust in our students and their ineffable drive and skill to learn.

It is time that we updated the way we approach the learning endeavor. "Delivering the curriculum" is the wrong way to describe the act of teaching (of fundamentally altering someone's worldview or habits of mind). "Learning outcomes" is the wrong language to understand what has happened when someone has learned. That person has changed. He or she has moved from one way of understanding and being to another. The person's qualitative alteration cannot be captured and characterized by just the end point. Instead we should be examining the journey of development—the trajectory of change. What happened along the way to evolve this person's perspectives? If you came up with the correct answer accidentally, does that show you understand? If you took very interesting steps but then reached an incorrect conclusion, does that count? Math teachers have been asking students for decades to show the work on the way to the solution. They are most interested in how the student arrived at the answer. We need to return to that wisdom in our assessments of student learning. We need to document and understand the progression of ideas and new understandings. There are no outcomes, because the learning is never finished.

Fits and starts characterize all learning and development. Before the greatest leaps in cognition, the learner will tend to seem the most disorganized, the most unclear or unsure. This is why law school students do their absolute worst writing in the first year, when they are just about to make a giant leap in intellectual understanding (Bean, 2011). Children's learning is far from linear. It is a complex, non-linear, dynamic system, which makes great leaps in chaotic manner. These miraculous jumps are what we must capture.

Prioritizing Experiences Over Artifacts

In this day and age of over-surveillance, there is a tendency to focus on showing what your students have learned using artifacts. Especially in the lower elementary grades, these adorable end products are loved by parents and school boards. I must admit, I experienced a sort of pre-nostalgia when my son,

Alexei, came home with the artifacts he made in kindergarten. "Oh how I will treasure these someday when he's grown," I thought. They would make nice decorations in our house, just as they decorated his classroom bulletin board. But the little paper owl represented little curiosity, exploration, or opportunity to learn. It may have been fun to trace and assemble the parts with glue and sparkles and feathers, but having seen him do similar obligatory class projects, I know that this owl was much more for my engagement and enjoyment than his. There were missed opportunities in this project—to invite children to be curious about real owls, to find out what the children wonder about owls, or even to have them reflect on the process of the experience as budding artists.

It was the day that Maggie's 2nd grade class was hanging the coral reef bulletin board. Parent-teacher conferences were coming up, and Ms. Bitoy was eager to impress them with the display. During silent reading, Ms. Bitoy pulled Maggie aside to let her know that she needed to finish her sea turtle for the coral reef—she hadn't yet colored the legs or put on the sequins. In complete sincerity, Maggie looked up from her book (Junie B. Jones, her favorite series) and asked, "Why?" For a second Ms. Bitoy was stunned, and she did not have a good answer for why a sea turtle needed colored legs or sequins on it. "It won't look as good on the board," was the actual reason, and didn't Maggie want her parents to like the work she had done when they visited that evening? Maggie's genuine concentration and intrinsic motivation were briskly thwarted, as she got the message that the work in the classroom was mainly for show. It is almost impossible for us as teachers to remember our frame of mind when we were experiencing our first insights as students. Research shows that individuals with more experience or expertise in any topic have a very difficult time putting themselves back in the shoes of novices (Bransford, Brown, & Cocking, 2000). That is why we must listen to what students are thinking and wondering. Questions are the exact tool for assessing where their true understanding lies.

The artifacts of learning are interesting, yes, but they cannot be allowed to trump the learning process itself. This is especially important when the lesson itself is the creation of the artifact and the process of creation is rote copying of a model or pattern. In the article "Gavin's Education," Shawna Nehiley

(2015) writes about discovering the box containing all of her son's schoolwork from the lower elementary grades. The box contained artwork and stories, laminated poster-sized colorful papers with her son's favorite colors, food, and hobbies displayed on them. As her son transitioned out of those years, she felt a pang of sadness that she would not be getting those adorable things coming home anymore. But as she reflected upon what genuine learning is, she discovered that the things were quite superficial.

> [Authentic] education is just too big for paper, too big for grades, and certainly too big for a poster board of facts and opinions. . . . [It] is so complete that sometimes the only way to see what your child is learning is to look between the lines. . . . I think this is because what he is now learning is how to grow into himself. I mean, how do you measure or record something as enormous as that? It doesn't happen in a neat straight line. It's much more of a circular process that keeps falling back in on itself. In order to see it happening at all you have to look in places no one ever taught you to look." (Nehiley, 2015)

Instead of the artifacts overshadowing the genuine experience, we can design the learning experience to overshadow the artifact, by letting the students decide how to showcase what they have learned. For the youngest children, this may involve giving them options ("How do you want to show the water cycle? Do you want to draw it, or mold it with clay, or act it out with some partners?"). After the representing stage, we are going to present our work to the class. As they gain in experience, children can be given a toolbox of options of how to represent their own learning. We can allow their divergent thinking be their guide. Do they want to write a comic book? A one-act play? Do they want to do an annotated bibliography? A sculpture? Do they want to give an oral report? Write a group blog post? Build a model?

For one of my final exams in graduate school, one of my professors set up an hour meeting with each of us. There was no format. He asked what we were going to take away from this course. We simply had a conversation, and based on the shared discussion, he was able to determine whether we had learned what he hoped from the course. He was also open to the idea that maybe we had learned other—equally valuable—things that he had never intended. Assessment can be enhanced (rather than diminished) when the process of representing their work is in the hands of the students. After all, assessment is truly about getting students to show what they have learned. Like letting them develop and ask their own questions, letting them decide how they will let you know they have learned can be a powerful experience in autonomy, self-expression, and curiosity.

Re-Centering on Student Learning

Curiosity learning goes far beyond simply transferring information from teachers' heads to students' notebooks. In the Banking Model of education, the teacher could simply write the facts in the notebook for the child and leave the middleman out of it (Finkel, 2000; Freire, 2000). But as we have seen, the focus on passive absorption—sitting through lectures, reading textbooks, and memorizing material before coughing it back up on a test—does not work.

On the other hand, in the curiosity classroom, the teacher shifts focus to the learner, encourages open-ended exploratory conversation, and facilitates a 'meeting of the minds' (Van Zee, 2000). In this approach, teachers are more like coaches, offering the students a focus, but not telling them how to think. As one teacher put it, "I had to switch from 'Here's your study guide, and here's your answer sheet' to 'How do you want to learn the content, and how can we support you?'" (Richmond, 2014).

When I prepared to teach my very first class, I chose a topic that I knew everything about: Comparative Perspectives on Language Development. I had just spent years researching how children learn to perceive language for my dissertation, had read every article or book ever written on the subject, and was recently crowned an "expert." I carefully chose each reading and assignment, and I was going to artfully "deliver the curriculum"—as if my truck would show up to dump a bunch of books and articles on them, and they would be thrilled at what they had received. It was the topic I knew the most about—and the course was the worst flop of my teaching career. I had stacked the deck, and there was nowhere for my students to enter into the dialogue. They would venture a guess at how the brain might work (like Sonia, searching for possibilities using her wonderful deductive reasoning) and I would tell them that they were wrong. They had had different experiences from mine and different ways of making meaning and knowledge. I was asking my students to behave and learn the way I wanted them to, to have a prescribed experience with the course and the information. But in the process, I forgot about them.

I now know that a Socratic stance (awareness of how little we really know or can know) can lead to genuine engagement. Only if I am a learner myself can my students and I meet in curiosity and co-create knowledge. After all, "To students, teachers are critically important role models because of what they are still learning, not because of what they already know. It is as experienced learners, with a high interest in, and high standards for knowledge and skills, that we communicate the lasting value of these things to students" (Fried, 2003, p. 48).

We can rest assured: Children are terrific learners. They spend every waking hour of every day growing in understanding of complex language and complex social situations: how to navigate the physical world, the social world, and their family dynamics; and how to hone their philosophies of life (Gopnik, 2009). Creating the curiosity classroom involves a degree of letting go of control and trusting that learning will happen. It is our job as teachers to support, maintain, revere, and expose curiosity in our students. We must protect their intrinsic motivation and exploration. We can use tools and techniques to guide, scaffold, connect, bridge, and remold their genuine interests toward the practice and process of inquiry. By constructing a curiosity classroom, we can channel our students' wonder and then widen it.

References

Alvarado, A. E., & Herr, P. R. (2003). *Inquiry-based learning using everyday objects: Hands-on instructional strategies that promote active learning in grades 3–8.* Thousand Oaks, CA: Corwin Press.

Amabile, T. A., & Gitomer, J. (1984). Children's artistic creativity: Effects of choice in task materials. *Personality and Social Psychology Bulletin, 10*(2), 209–215.

Amabile, T. M., & Hennessey, B. A. (1992). The motivation for creativity in children. In A. K. Boggiano & T. S. Pittman (Eds.), *Achievement and motivation: A social-developmental perspective* (pp. 54–76). Cambridge, England: Cambridge University Press.

Anderson, M. (2016). *Learning to choose, choosing to learn: The key to student motivation.* Alexandria, VA: ASCD.

Anderson, R. C., Shirley, L. L., Wilson, P. T., & Fielding, L. G. (1987). Interestingness of children's reading material. In R. E. Snow & M. J. Farr (Eds.), *Aptitude, learning and instruction: Vol. 3. Cognitive and affective process analyses.* Hillsdale, NJ: Erlbaum.

Andrade, J. (2010). What does doodling do? *Applied Cognitive Psychology, 24*(1), 100–106.

Arendt, H. (1961). *Between past and future.* New York: Penguin Books.

Aristotle. (1947). Metaphysics. In R. McKeon (Ed.), *Introduction to Aristotle* (pp. 238–296). New York: Modern Library.

Ashton-Warner, S. (2003). Creative teaching. In *The Jossey-Bass reader on teaching* (pp. 152–165). San Francisco, CA: Jossey-Bass.

Atwell, N. (2015, September). Keynote speech. Clinton Global Initiative Topic Dinner, New York. Retrieved from http://www.globalteacherprize.org/3-life-changing-lessons-from-teacher-prize-winner-nancie-atwells-keynote-at-cgi

Ayers, W. (2003). The mystery of teaching. In *The Jossey-Bass reader on teaching* (pp. 26–37). San Francisco, CA: Jossey-Bass.

Barker, J. E., Semenov, A. D., Michaelson, L., Provan, L. S., Snyder, H. R., & Munakata, Y. (2014). Less-structured time in children's daily lives predicts self-directed executive functioning. *Frontiers in Psychology | Developmental Psychology, 5*(593), 1–16.

Barnett, L. A. (1984). Research note: Young children's resolution of distress through play. *Journal of Child Psychology and Psychiatry, 25*(3), 477–483.

Barrett, P., Zhang, U., Moffat, J., & Kobbacy, K. (2013). A holistic, multi-level analysis identifying the impact of classroom design on pupils' learning. *Building and Environment, 59*(5), 678–689.

Barrett, T. (2015, February 26). Convene your classroom creative council [blog post]. Retrieved from *The Curious Creator* at http://edte.ch/blog/2015/02/26/convene-your-classroom-creative-council/

Barron, F. (1988). Putting creativity to work. In R. J. Sternberg (Ed.), *The nature of creativity: Contemporary psychological perspectives* (pp. 76–98). Cambridge, England: Cambridge University Press.

Barrows, T. S., Ager, S. M., Bennett, M. F., Braun, H. I., Clark, J. L. D., Harris, L. G., & Klein, S. F. (1981). *College students' knowledge and beliefs: A survey of global understanding: The final report of the Global Understanding Project.* New Rochelle, NY: Change Magazine Press.

Bauerlein, M. (2008). *The dumbest generation: How the digital age stupefies young Americans and jeopardizes our future (or, don't trust anyone under 30).* New York: Penguin.

Bean, J. C. (2011). *Engaging ideas: The professor's guide to integrating writing, critical thinking, and active learning in the classroom* (2nd ed.). San Francisco, CA: Jossey-Bass.

Bedell, G. (1980). *Philosophizing with Socrates: An introduction to the study of philosophy.* Lanham, MD: University Press of America.

Belton, T. (2001). Television and imagination: An investigation of the medium's influence on children's storymaking. *Media, Culture and Society, 23*(6), 799–820.

Belton, T. (2013, March 27). Feeling bored? Make something of it! [blog post]. Retrieved from http://www.huffingtonpost.co.uk/dr-teresa-belton/easter-feeling-bored-make-something_b_2962848.html?utm_hp_ref=uk

Belton, T., & Priyadharshini, E. (2007). Boredom and schooling: A cross-disciplinary exploration. *Cambridge Journal of Education, 37*(4), 579–595.

Berger, W. (2014). *A more beautiful question: The power of inquiry to spark breakthrough ideas.* New York: Bloomsbury.

Berlyne, D. E. (1966). Curiosity and exploration. *Science, 153*(3731), 25–33.

Best, J. R., Miller, P. H., & Naglieri, J. A. (2011). Relations between executive function and academic achievement from ages 5 to 17 in a large, representative national sample. *Learning Individual Differences, 21*(4), 327–336.

Bissell, J. M. (2004). Teachers' construction of space and place: The method in the madness. *Forum, 46*(1), 28–32.

Blair, C., & Razza, R. P. (2007). Relating effortful control, executive function, and false belief understanding to emerging math and literacy ability in kindergarten. *Child Development, 78*(2), 647–663.

Booth, E. (2001). *The everyday work of art: Awakening the extraordinary in your daily life.* Lincoln, NE: iUniverse.

Bornstein, M. H., Hahn, C. S., & Suwalsky, J. T. (2013). Physically developed and explor-atory young infants contribute to their own long-term academic achievement. *Psychological Science, 24*(10), 1906–1917.

Boubekri, M., Cheung, I. N., Reid, K. J., Wang, C. H., & Zee, P. C. (2014). Impact of windows and daylight exposure on overall health and sleep quality of office workers: A case-control pilot study. *Journal of Clinical Sleep Medicine, 10*(6), 603–611.

Bouldin, P. (2006). An investigation of the fantasy predisposition and fantasy style of children with imaginary companions. *Journal of Genetic Psychology, 167*(1), 17–29.

Bransford, J. D., Brown, A. L., & Cocking, R. R. (Eds.). (2000). *How people learn: Brain, mind, experience, and school.* Washington, DC: National Academy Press.

Brehm, A. E. (2015). *Brehm's life of animals: A complete natural history for popular home instruction and for the use of schools* (R. Schmidtlein, Trans.). London: Forgotten Books. (Original work published 1864)

Brewer, C. (1995). *Music and learning: Seven ways to use music in the classroom.* Brookline, MA: Zephyr Press.

Brill, F. (2004). Thinking outside the box: Imagination and empathy beyond story writing. *Literacy, 38*(2), 83–89.

Bronson, P., & Merryman, A. (2010, July 10). The creativity crisis. *Newsweek.* Retrieved from http://www.newsweek.com/creativity-crisis-74665

Bruce, T. (1991). *Time to play in early childhood education.* London: Hodder & Stoughton.

Bruner, J. S. (1966). *Toward a theory of instruction.* Cambridge, MA: Harvard University Press.

Bunting, A. (2004). Secondary schools designed for a purpose—But which one? *Teacher, 154,* 10–13.

Burroughs, J. (1919). *Field and study.* Cambridge, MA: Riverside Press.

Cameron, C. E., Brock, L. L., Murrah, W. M., Bell, L. H., Worzalla, S. L., Grissmer, D., & Morrison, F. J. (2012). Fine motor skills and executive function both con-tribute to kindergarten achievement. *Child Development, 83*(4), 1229–1244. doi: 10.1111/j.1467- 8624.2012.01768.x

Carnevale, A. P., Gainer, L. J., & Meltzer, A. S. (1990). *Workplace basics: The essential skills employers want.* San Francisco: Jossey-Bass.

Carr, D. (1998). The art of asking questions in the teaching of science. *School Science Review, 79*(289), 47–60.

Carroll, L. (2006). *Alice's adventures in wonderland & through the looking-glass.* New York: Bantam Dell. (Original work published 1865)

Chi, M. T. H., Bassok, M., Lewis, M. W., Reimann, P., & Glaser, R. (1989). Self-explanations: How students study and use examples in learning to solve problems. *Cognitive Science, 13*(2), 145–182.

Chouinard, M. M., Harris, P. L., & Maratsos, M. P. (2007). Children's questions: A mechanism for cognitive development. *Monographs of the Society for Research in Child Development, 72*(1), 1–129.

Cicero, M. T. (1914). *De finibus bonorum et malorum* (H. Rackham, Trans.). Cambridge, MA: Harvard University Press.

Cifone, M. V. (2013). Questioning and learning: How do we recognize children's questions? *Curriculum & Teaching Dialogue, 15*(1-2), 41–55.

Clyde, J. A., & Condon, M. W. F. (2000). *Get real: Bringing kids' learning lives into the classroom.* York, ME: Stenhouse Publishers.

Csikszentmihalyi, M. (1997). *Finding flow: The psychology of engagement with everyday life.* New York: Basic Books.

Csikszentmihalyi, M. (2000). *Beyond boredom and anxiety: Experiencing flow in work and play (25th anniversary ed.).* San Francisco, CA: Jossey-Bass.

Curtis, D., & Carter, M. (2015). *Designs for living and learning: Transforming early childhood environments* (2nd ed.). St. Paul, MN: Redleaf Press.

d'Ailly, H. (2003). Children's autonomy and perceived control in learning: A model of motivation and achievement in Taiwan. *Journal of Educational Psychology, 95*(1), 84–96.

d'Ailly, H. (2004). The role of choice in children's learning: A distinctive cultural and gender difference in efficacy, interest, and effort. *Canadian Journal of Behavioural Science, 36*(1), 17–29.

Darden, D. (1999). Boredom: A socially disvalued emotion. *Sociological Spectrum, 19*(1), 13–37.

Darwin, C. (1874). *The descent of man: And selection in relation to sex* (Rev. edition.). Philadelphia, PA: J. Wanamaker.

Dawley, H. (2006, April 30). In praise of boredom, sweet boredom: A researcher believes it can be good for us. Retrieved from http://www.medialifemagazine.com /in-praise-of-boredom-sweet-boredom/

Day, D.R. (1995). *Environmental law: Fundamentals for schools.* Alexandria, VA: National School Boards Association.

de Charms, R. (1968). *Personal causation.* New York: Academic Press.

de Charms, R. (1976). *Enhancing motivation: Change in the classroom.* New York: Irvington.

Deci, E. L. (1975). *Intrinsic motivation.* New York: Plenum.

Deci, E. L., Koestner, R., & Ryan, R. M. (2001). Extrinsic rewards and intrinsic motivation in education: Reconsidered once again. *Review of Educational Research, 71*(1), 1–27.

Deci, E. L., & Ryan, R. M. (1985). *Intrinsic motivation and self-determination in human behavior.* New York: Plenum.

de Manzano, Ö., Theorell, T., Harmat, L., & Ullén, F. (2010). The psychophysiology of flow during piano playing. *Emotion, 10*(3), 301–311.

Deviny, J., Duncan, S., Harris, S., Rody, M. A., & Rosenberry, L. (2010). *Inspiring spaces for young children.* Lewisville, NC: Gryphon House.

Dewey, J. (1909). *Moral principles in education.* New York: Houghton Mifflin.

Dewey, J. (1916). *Democracy and education: An introduction to the philosophy of education.* New York: Macmillan.

Diachenko, O. M. (2011). On major developments in preschoolers' imaginations. *International Journal of Early Years Education, 19*(1), 19–25.

Diamond, A. (1995). Evidence of robust recognition memory early in life even when assessed by reaching behavior. *Journal of Experimental Child Psychology, 59*(3), 419–456.

Dichter, B. (2014, October 6). Teaching metacognition: Insight into how your students think is key to high achievement in all domains. Retrieved from http://www.opencolleges.edu.au/informed/features/the-importance-of-metacognition/#ixzz3FfxIKwJf

Dillon, J. T. (1983). *Teaching and the art of questioning.* Bloomington, IN: Phi Delta Kappa Educational Foundation.

Doorley, S., & Witthoft, S. (2012). *Make space: How to set the stage for creative collaboration.* Hoboken, NJ: John Wiley & Sons.

Dori, Y. J., & Herscovitz, O. (1999). Question posing capability as an alternative evaluation method: Analysis of an environmental case study. *Journal of Research in Science Teaching, 36*(4), 411–430.

Dweck, C. S. (1999). *Self-theories.* Philadelphia: Psychology Press.

Dweck, C. S. (2006). *Mindset: The new psychology of success.* New York: Random House.

Dyer, J., Gregersen, H., & Christensen, C. M. (2011). *The innovator's DNA: Mastering the five skills of disruptive innovators.* Boston: Harvard Business Review Press.

Earthman, G. I. (2004). Prioritization of 31 criteria for school building adequacy. American Civil Liberties Union Foundation of Maryland. Retrieved from http://www.schoolfunding.info/policy/facilities/ACLUfacilities_report1-04.pdf

Edwards, C. (1993). Partner, nurturer, and guide: The roles of the Reggio teacher in action. In C. Edwards, L. Gandini, & G. Foreman (Eds.), *The hundred languages of children: The Reggio Emilia approach to early childhood education.* Norwood, NJ: Ablex.

Egan, K. (1989). *Teaching as story telling: An alternative approach to teaching and curriculum in elementary school.* Chicago: University of Chicago Press.

Egan, K. (1997). *The educated mind: How cognitive tools shape our understanding.* Chicago: University of Chicago Press.

Einstein, A. (1949, March 13). Einstein Says 'It Is Miracle' Inquiry Is Not 'Strangled.' *New York Times.*

Eliot, T. S. (1943). *Four quartets.* New York: Harcourt.

Emerson, R. W. (1850). *Representative men: Seven lectures.* Cambridge, MA: Belknap Press.

Engel, S. (2011). Children's need to know: Curiosity in schools. *Harvard Educational Review, 81*(4), 625–645.

Engel, S., & Labella, M. (2011). *Encouraging exploration: The effects of teaching behavior on student expressions of curiosity*. (Unpublsished honors thesis). Williams College.

Engel, S., & Randall, K. (2009). How teachers respond to children's inquiry. *American Educational Research Journal, 46*(1), 183–202.

Falchi, F., Cinzano, P., Elvidge, C. D., Keith, D. M., & Haim, A. (2011). Limiting the impact of light pollution on human health, environment, and stellar visibility. *Journal of Environmental Management, 92*(10), 2714–2722.

Fazey, D. M. A., & Fazey, J. A. (2001). The potential for autonomy in learning: Perceptions of competence, motivation, and locus of control in first-year undergraduate students. *Studies in Higher Education, 26*(3), 345–361.

Feynman, R. P. (2006). *Perfectly reasonable deviations from the beaten track*. New York: Basic Books.

Fielding, R. (2006, March 1). What they see is what we get: A primer on light [blog post]. Retrieved from Edutopia at http://www.edutopia.org/what-they-see-what-we-get

Fink, J. (2015, Feb 19). Why schools are failing our boys. *Washington Post*. http://www .washingtonpost.com/news/parenting/wp/2015/02/19/why-schools-are-failing -our-boys/?tid=sm_fb

Finkel, D. L. (2000). *Teaching with your mouth shut*. Portsmouth, NH: Heinemann.

Fisher, J. (2013). *Starting from the child: Teaching and learning from 4 to 8* (4th ed.). Buckingham, England: Open University Press.

Fivush, R. (2008). Sociocultural perspectives on autobiographical memory. In M. Courage & N. Cowan (Eds.). *The development of memory in children*. New York: Psychology Press.

Foucault, M. (1982). The subject and power. Afterword to H. L. Dreyfus & P. Rabinow, *Michel Foucault: Beyond structuralism and hermeneutics*. Brighton, UK: Harvester.

Freire, P. (1998). *Pedagogy of freedom: Ethics, democracy, and civic courage*. Lanham, MD: Rowman & Littlefield.

Freire, P. (2000). *Pedagogy of the oppressed*. New York: Continuum.

French, H. W. (2001, February 25). More sunshine for Japan's overworked students. *New York Times*, p. 18.

Fried, R. L. (2003). Passionate teaching. In *The Jossey-Bass reader on teaching* (pp. 38–51). San Francisco, CA: Jossey-Bass.

Gadamer, H.G. (1975). *Truth and method*. London: Bloomsbury Academic.

Garner, R., Brown, R., Sanders, S., & Menke, D. J. (1992). "Seductive details" and learning from text. In K. A. Renninger, S. Hidi, & A. Krapp (Eds.), *The role of interest in learning and development* (pp. 239–254). Hillsdale, NJ: Erlbaum.

Gaskins, S., & Paradise, R. (2010). Learning through observation in daily life. In D. F. Lancy, J. Bock, & S. Gaskins (Eds.), *The anthropology of learning in childhood* (pp. 85–118). Lanham, MD: AltaMira Press.

Gibson, J.J. (1950). *The perception of the visual world*. Boston: Houghton Mifflin.

Goldstein, A., & Russ, S. W. (2000). Understanding children's literature and its relationship to fantasy ability and coping. *Imagination, Cognition, and Personality, 20*(2), 105–126.

Golinkoff, R., & Hirsh-Pasek, K., with Eyer, D. (2003). *Einstein never used flash cards: How our children really learn—and why they need to play more and memorize less.* Emmaus, PA: Rodale Books.

Goncu, A., Jain, J., & Tuermer, U. (2007). Children's play as cultural interpretation. In A. Goncu & S. Gaskins (Eds.), *Play and development: Evolutionary, sociocultural, and functional perspectives* (pp. 155–178). New York: Lawrence Erlbaum.

Goodman, Y. (1978). Kidwatching: An alternative to testing. *National Elementary Principal, 57,* 41–45.

Goodwin, B. (2014). Research says curiosity is fleeting, but teachable. *Educational Leadership, 72*(1), 73–74.

Gopnik, A. (2009). *The philosophical baby: What children's minds tell us about truth, love, and the meaning of life.* New York: Farrar, Straus and Giroux.

Gordon, T. (1989). *Teaching children self-discipline at home and at school.* New York: Times Books.

Goyal, N. (2012). *One size does not fit all: A student's assessment of school.* Roslyn Heights, NY: Alternative Education Resource Organization.

Gray, P. (2012, February 28). The benefits of unschooling: Report I from a large survey [blog post]. Retrieved from *Freedom to Learn* at https://www.psychologytoday.com/blog/freedom-learn/201202/the-benefits-unschooling-report-i-large-survey

Gray, P. (2013). *Free to learn: Why unleashing the instinct to play will make our children happier, more self-reliant, and better students for life.* New York: Basic Books.

Greene, L. (2005). Questioning questions. *The National Teaching & Learning Forum, 14*(2), 1–3.

Greene, M. (1995). *Releasing the imagination: Essays on education, the arts, and social change.* San Francisco, CA: Jossey-Bass.

Grossman, S. (2008). Offering children choices. Retrieved from http://www.earlychildhoodnews.com/earlychildhood/article_view.aspx?ArticleID=607

Gruber, M. J., Gelman, B. D., & Ranganath, C. (2014). States of curiosity modulate hippocampus-dependent learning via the dopaminergic circuit. *Neuron, 84*(2), 486–496.

Gunderson, E. A., Gripshover, S. J., Romero, C., Dweck, C. S., Goldin-Meadow, S., & Levine, S. C. (2013). Parent praise to 1- to 3-year-olds predicts children's motivational frameworks 5 years later. *Child Development, 84*(5), 1526–1541.

Gupta, R. (2012). *The effects of ventromedial prefrontal cortex damage on interpersonal coordination in social interaction.* (Unpublished doctoral dissertation). University of Iowa, Iowa City. Retrieved from http://ir.uiowa.edu/etd/2883.

Heidegger, M. (1995). *The fundamental concepts of metaphysics: World, finitude, solitude* (W. McNeill & N. Walker, Trans.). Bloomington, IN: Indiana University Press.

Hensch, T. K. (2004). Critical period regulation. *Annual Review of Neuroscience, 27,* 549–579.

Henderlong, J., & Lepper, M. R. (2002). The effects of praise on children's intrinsic motivation: A review and synthesis. *Psychological Bulletin, 128*(5), 774–795.

Hershong Mahone Group. (2003). *Windows and classrooms: A study of student performance and the indoor environment.* Retrieved from http://h-m-g.com/projects /daylighting/summaries%20on%20daylighting.htm

Hetland, L., Winner, E., Veenema, S., & Sheridan, K. M. (2007). *Studio thinking: The real benefits of visual arts education.* New York: Teachers College Press.

Hewlett, B. S., Fouts, H. N., Boyette, A. H., & Hewlett, B. L. (2011). Social learning among Congo Basin hunter-gatherers. *Philosophical Transactions B, 366*(1567), 1168–1178.

Higgins, S., Hall, E., Wall, K., Woolner, P., & McCaughey, C. (2005). *The impact of school environments: A literature review.* The Centre for Learning and Teaching, School of Education, Communication, and Language Science, University of Newcastle. Retrieved from http://www.ncl.ac.uk/cflat/news/DCReport.pdf

Holmes, R. M., Pellegrini, A. D., & Schmidt, S. L. (2006). The effects of different recess timing regimens on preschoolers' classroom attention. *Early Child Development and Care, 176*(7), 735–743.

Holt, J. (1983). *How children learn.* Rev. ed. New York: Da Capo Press.

Holt, M. (2002). It's time to start the slow school movement. *Phi Delta Kappan, 84*(4), 264–271.

Hopkins, E. J., Dore, R. A., & Lillard, A. S. (2015). Do children learn from pretense? *Journal of Experimental Child Psychology, 130*(3), 1–18.

Horne, M. (2004). Breaking down the school walls. *Forum, 46*(1), 6.

Hunsberger, M. (1992). The time of texts. In W. F. Pinar & W. M. Reynolds (Eds.), *Understanding curriculum as phenomenological and deconstructed text* (pp. 64–91). New York: Teachers College Press.

Hunt, S. D., Chonko, L. B., & Wood, V. R. (1986). Marketing education and marketing success: Are they related? *Journal of Marketing Education, 8*(2), 2–13.

Hunter, J. P., & Csikszentmihalyi, M. (2003). The positive psychology of interested adolescents. *Journal of Youth and Adolescence, 32*(1), 27–35.

Imus, D. (2008). *Growing up green: Baby and child care.* New York: Simon & Schuster.

Jacobs, J. (1961). *The death and life of great American cities.* New York: Random House.

Jepma, M., Verdonschot, R. G., van Steenbergen, H., Rombouts, S. A. R. B., & Nieuwenhuis, S. (2012). Neural mechanisms underlying the induction and relief of perceptual curiosity. *Frontiers in Behavioral Neuroscience, 6,* 100–104.

Johnson, C. (2005). *Harold and the purple crayon.* New York: HarperCollins.

Johnson, J. S., & Newport, E. L. (1989). Critical period effects in second language learning: The influence of maturational state on the acquisition of English as a second language. *Cognitive Psychology, 21*(1), 60–99.

Johnson, S. (1825). *The works of Samuel Johnson, LL.D.* Oxford, England: Talboys and Wheeler and W. Pickering.

Kamins, M. L., & Dweck, C. S. (1999). Person versus process praise and criticism: Implications for contingent self-worth and coping. *Developmental Psychology, 35*(3), 835–847.

Kast, A., & Connor, K. (1988). Sex and age differences in responses to informational and controlling feedback. *Personality and Social Psychology Bulletin, 14*(3), 514–523.

Kaufman, S.B. (2013, December 10). Conversation on daydreaming with Jerome L. Singer [blog post]. Retrieved from *Beautiful Minds* at http://blogs.scientificamerican.com/beautiful-minds/conversation-on-daydreaming-with-jerome-l-singer/

Kelly, G. A. (1963). *A theory of personality: The psychology of personal constructs.* New York: W. W. Norton and Company.

King, A. (1994). Autonomy and question asking: The role of personal control in guided student-generated questioning. *Learning and Individual Differences, 6*(2), 163–185.

Kirkpatrick, E. A. (1903/2009). *Fundamentals of child study.* New York: MacMillan.

Klatte, M., Bergstroem, K., & Lachmann, T. (2013). Does noise affect learning? A short review on noise effects on cognitive performance in children. *Frontiers in Psychology, 4,* 1–6.

Knudsen, E. I. (2004). Sensitive periods in the development of the brain and behavior. *Journal of Cognitive Neuroscience, 16*(8), 1412–1425.

Kohn, A. (1993). Choices for children: Why and how to let students decide. *Phi Delta Kappan, 75*(1), 8–21.

Kohn, A. (1999). *Punished by rewards: The trouble with gold stars, incentive plans, A's, praise, and other bribes.* New York: Houghton Mifflin.

Kohn, A. (2011). "Well, duh!" Ten obvious truths that we shouldn't be ignoring. *American School Board Journal.*

Kohn, D. (2015, May 16). Let the kids learn through play. *New York Times.* Retrieved from http://www.nytimes.com/2015/05/17/opinion/sunday/let-the-kids-learn-through-play.html?_r=1

Kounios, J., & Beeman, M. (2009). The aha! moment: The cognitive neuroscience of insight. *Current Directions in Psychological Science, 18*(4), 210–216.

Kuhl, P. K. (2004). Early language acquisition: Cracking the speech code. *Nature Reviews Neuroscience, 5*(11), 831–843.

Kuhl, P. K., & Rivera-Gaxiola, M. (2008). Neural substrates of language acquisition. *Annual Review of Neuroscience, 31,* 511–534.

Kuhn, D., & Ho, V. (1980). Self-directed activity and cognitive development. *Journal of Applied Developmental Psychology, 1*(2), 119–133.

Kumar, M. (2008). *Dictionary of quotations.* New Delhi, India: APH Publishing Corporation.

Lachman, S. J. (1997). Learning is a process: Toward an improved definition of learning. *Journal of Psychology: Interdisciplinary and Applied, 131*(5), 477–480.

Land, G., & Jarman, B. (1993). *Breakpoint and beyond: Mastering the future—today.* Champaign, IL: HarperBusiness

Lehman, J., & Stanley, K. O. (2011). Abandoning objectives: Evolution through the search for novelty alone. *Evolutionary Computation, 19*(2), 189–223.

Lepper, M. R., Greene, D., & Nisbett, R. E. (1973). Undermining children's intrinsic interest with extrinsic rewards: A test of the "overjustification" hypothesis. *Journal of Personality and Social Psychology, 28*(1), 129–137.

Leslie, I. (2014). *Curious: The desire to know and why your future depends on it.* New York: Basic Books.

Levy, A. K., Wolfgang, C. H., & Koorland, M. A. (1992). Sociodramatic play as a method for enhancing the language performance of kindergarten age students. *Early Childhood Research Quarterly, 7*(2), 245–262.

Lewis, H. R. (2001). *Slow down: Getting more out of Harvard by doing less.* Retrieved from http://scholar.harvard.edu/files/harrylewis/files/slowdown2004.pdf

Lickona, T. (1991). *Educating for character: How our schools can teach respect and responsibility.* New York: Bantam.

Lillard, A. S. (2005). *Montessori: The science behind the genius.* New York: Oxford University Press.

Lillard, A., & Else-Quest, N. (2006). Evaluating Montessori education. *Science, 313*(5795), 1893–1894.

Limb, C. J., & Braun, A. R. (2008). Neural substrates of spontaneous musical performance: an FMRI study of jazz improvisation. *PLoS One, 3*(2), 1679.

Lipton, J. S., & Spelke, E. S. (2003). Origins of number sense: Large-number discrimination in human infants. *Psychological Science, 14*(5), 396–401.

Lobel, A. (1979). *Frog and toad together.* New York: Harpercollins.

Loewenstein, G. (1994). The psychology of curiosity: A review and reinterpretation. *Psychological Bulletin, 116*(1), 75–98.

Lowry, N., & Johnson, D. W. (1981). Effects of controversy on epistemic curiosity, achievement, and attitudes. *Journal of Social Psychology, 115*(1), 31–43.

Lucas, C. G., Bridgers, S., Griffiths, T. L., & Gopnik, A. (2014). When children are better (or at least more open-minded) learners than adults: Developmental differences in learning the forms of causal relationships. *Cognition, 131*(2), 284–299.

Luria, A. R. (1961). *The role of speech in the regulation of normal and abnormal behavior.* New York: Liveright.

Mangels, J. A., Butterfield, B., Lamb, J., Good, C., & Dweck, C. S. (2006). Why do beliefs about intelligence influence learning success? A social cognitive neuroscience model. *Social Cognitive and Affective Neuroscience, 1*(2), 75–86.

Mar, R. A. (2011). The neural bases of social cognition and story comprehension. *Annual Review of Psychology, 62*(1), 103–134.

Mar, R. A., Tackett, J. L., & Moore, C. (2010). Exposure to media and theory-of-mind development in preschoolers. *Cognitive Development, 25*(2), 69–78.

Marbach, E. S., & Yawkey, T. D. (1980). The effects of imaginative play actions on language development in five-year-old children. *Psychology in the Schools, 17*(2), 257–263.

McCombs, B. (2015). Developing responsible and autonomous learners: A key to motivating students. Retrieved from http://www.apa.org/education/k12/learners.aspx

McCraven, V. G., Singer, J. L., & Wilensky, H. (1956). Delaying capacity, fantasy, and planning ability: A factorial study of some basic ego functions. *Journal of Consulting Psychology, 20*(5), 375–383.

McGraw, P., & Warren, C. (2010). Benign violations: Making immoral behavior funny. *Psychological Science, 21*(8), 1141–1149.

McGregor, J. (2004). Space, power, and the classroom. *Forum, 46*(1), 13–18.

McNamara, D., & Waugh, D. (1993). Classroom organisation: A discussion of grouping strategies in the light of the "Three wise men's" report. *School Organisation, 13*(1), 41–50.

McNerney, S. (2012). Relaxation and creativity: The science of sleeping on it [blog post]. Retrieved from http://bigthink.com/insights-of-genius/relaxation-creativity-the-science-of-sleeping-on-it

McRobbie, C., & Tobin, K. (1997). A social constructivist perspective on learning environments. *International Journal of Science Education, 19*(2), 193–208.

McWilliams, P. (2003). Learning to read. In *The Jossey-Bass reader on teaching* (pp. 77–79). San Francisco, CA: Jossey-Bass.

Mead, M. (1970). *Culture and commitment: A study of the generation gap.* London: The Bodley Head.

Medina, J. (2014). *Brain rules: 12 principles for surviving and thriving at work, home, and school* (Updated and expanded ed.). Seattle, WA: Pear Press.

Meyer, D. K., & Turner, J. C. (2002). Discovering emotion in classroom motivation research. *Educational Psychologist, 37*(2), 107–114.

Miller, M. (2014, January 30). Twenty useful ways to use TodaysMeet in schools [blog post]. Retrieved from *Ditch That Textbook* at http://ditchthattextbook.com/2014/01/30/20-useful-ways-to-use-todaysmeet-in-schools/

Mitra, S. (2006). *The hole in the wall: Self-organising systems in education.* New York: McGraw-Hill.

Mitra, S. (2007, February). *Kids can teach themselves* [Video file]. Retrieved from https://www.ted.com/talks/sugata_mitra_shows_how_kids_teach_themselves?language=en

Montessori, M. (1989). *To educate the human potential.* Oxford: Clio Press.

Montgomery, L. M. (1976). *Anne of Green Gables.* New York: Bantam Books. (Original work published 1908)

Moore, S. G., & Bulbulian, K. N. (1976). The effects of contrasting styles of adult-child interaction on children's curiosity. *Developmental Psychology, 12*(2), 171–172.

Morgan, N., & Saxton, J. (2006). *Asking better questions* (2nd ed.). Ontario, Canada: Pembroke Publishers.

Moser, J. S., Schroder, H. S., Heeter, C., Moran, T. P., & Lee, Y-H. (2011). Mind your errors: Evidence for a neural mechanism linking growth mind-set to adaptive posterror adjustments. *Psychological Science, 22*(12), 1484–1489.

Muller, J. (2014). What impact has dopamine had on human evolution? Retrieved from https://www.quora.com/What-impact-has-dopamine-had-on-human-evolution

Mueller, C. M., & Dweck, C. S. (1998). Praise for intelligence can undermine children's motivation and performance. *Journal of Personality and Social Psychology, 75*(1), 33–52.

Naiman, L. (2014, June 6). Can creativity be taught? Results from research studies. Retrieved from https://www.creativityatwork.com/2012/03/23/can-creativity-be-taught/

National Commission on Excellence in Education. (1983). A nation at risk: The imperative for educational reform. Washington, DC: Government Printing Office.

Nehiley, S. (2015, April 20). Gavin's education [blog post]. Retrieved from *Sudbury Valley School Blog* at http://blog.sudburyvalley.org/2015/04/gavins-education/

Newton, P., Driver, R., & Osborne, J. (1999). The place of argumentation in the pedagogy of school science. *International Journal of Science Education, 21*(5), 553–576.

Nolen, S. B. (2001). Constructing literacy in the kindergarten: Task structure, collaboration, and motivation. *Cognition and Instruction, 19*(1), 95–142.

Opdal, P. M. (2001). Curiosity, wonder, and education seen as perspective development. *Studies in Philosophy and Education, 20*(4), 331–344.

Oppenheimer, R. J. (2001). Increasing student motivation and facilitating learning. *College Teaching, 49*(3), 96–98.

Orr, D. W. (2010). Foreword. In *The third teacher: 79 ways you can use design to transform teaching and learning.* New York: Harry N. Abrams.

Ostroff, W. L. (2012). *Understanding how young children learn: Bringing the science of child development to the classroom.* Alexandria, VA: ASCD.

Ostroff, W. L. (2014). Don't just sit there . . . pay attention! *Educational Leadership, 72*(2), 70–74.

Ostroff, W. L. (2015). Asking to learn. *Educational Leadership, 73*(1). Retrieved from http://www.ascd.org/publications/educational-leadership/sept15/vol73/num01/Asking-to-Learn.aspx

Palmer, P. J. (2003). The heart of a teacher: Identity and integrity in teaching. In *The Jossey-Bass reader on teaching* (pp. 3–25). San Francisco, CA: Jossey-Bass.

Pappano, L. (2014, February 9). Learning to think differently. *New York Times.* Education Life, 8–10.

Pascual-Leone, A., Nguyet, D., Cohen, L. G., Brasil-Neto, J. P., Cammarota, A., & Hallett, M. (1995). Modulation of muscle responses evoked by transcranial magnetic stimulation during the acquisition of new fine motor skills. *Journal of Neurophysiology, 74*(3), 1037–1045.

Paul, R., & Elder, L. (2007). *The thinker's guide to the art of Socratic questioning.* Tomales, CA: The Foundation for Critical Thinking.

Pedrosa de Jesus, H., Almeida, P., & Watts, M. (2004). Questioning styles and students' learning: Four case studies. *Educational Psychology, 24*(4), 531–548.

Pedrosa de Jesus, H. T., Almeida, P. A., Teixeira-Dias, J. J., & Watts, M. (2006). Students' questions: Building a bridge between Kolb's learning styles and approaches to learning. *Education & Training, 48*(2/3), 97–111.

Perry, B.D. (2001). Curiosity: The fuel of development. *Early Childhood Today.* Retrieved from http://teacher.scholastic.com/professional/bruceperry/curiosity.htm

Piaget, J. (1973). *Main trends in psychology.* London: George Allen & Unwin.

Pincock, S. (2004). Francis Harry Compton Crick. *The Lancet, 364,* 576.

Pisula, W. (2009). *Curiosity and information seeking in animal and human behavior.* Boca Raton, FL: Brown Walker Press.

Pisula, W., Turlejski, K., & Charles, E. P. (2013). Comparative psychology as unified psychology: The case of curiosity and other novelty-related behavior. *Review of General Psychology, 17*(2), 224–229.

Plato. (2006). *The Republic* (R. E. Allen, Trans.). New Haven, CT: Yale University Press.

Post, P. G., & Wrisberg, C. A. (2012). A phenomenological investigation of gymnasts' lived experience of imagery. *The Sport Psychologist, 26*(1), 98–121.

Post, P. G., Wrisberg, C. A., & Mullins, S. (2010). A field test of the influence of pre-game imagery on basketball free throw shooting. *Journal of Imagery Research in Sport and Physical Activity, 5*(1).

Postman, N. (1979). *Teaching as a conserving activity.* New York: Delacorte Press.

Postman, N. (1999). *Building a bridge to the 18th century: How the past can improve our future.* New York: Alfred A. Knopf.

Raine, A., Reynolds, C., Venables, P. H., & Mednick, S. A. (2002). Stimulation seeking and intelligence: A prospective longitudinal study. *Journal of Personality and Social Psychology, 82*(4), 663–674.

Rainey, R. G. (1965). The effects of directed versus non-directed laboratory work on high school chemistry achievement. *Journal of Research in Science Teaching, 3*(4), 286–92.

Ranganathan, V. K., Siemionow, V., Liu, J. Z., Sahgal, V., & Yue, G. H. (2004). From mental power to muscle power—Gaining strength by using the mind. *Neuropsychologia, 42,* 944–956.

Reeve, J., Nix, G., & Hamm, D. (2003). Testing models of the experience of self-determination in intrinsic motivation and the conundrum of choice. *Journal of Educational Psychology, 95*(2), 375–392.

Renninger, K. A., & Hidi, S. (2002). Student interest and achievement: Developmental issues raised by a case study. In A. Wigfield & J. S. Eccles (Eds.), *Development of achievement motivation* (pp. 173–195). San Diego, CA: Academic Press.

Rey, H. A., & Rey, M. (1941). *Curious George.* New York: Houghton Mifflin Harcourt.

Richmond, E. (2014, October 24). Putting students in charge to close the achievement gap. Retrieved from http://hechingerreport.org/content/putting-students-charge-close-achievement-gap_17676/

Rilke, R. M. (1934). *Letters to a young poet*. New York: W. W. Norton.

Ritchie, A. I. T. (1885|2008). *Mrs. Dymond*. Charleston, SC: Bibliolife.

Rogoff, B. (1990). *Apprenticeships in thinking: Cognitive development in social context*. New York: Oxford University Press.

Romberg, A. R., & Saffran, J. R. (2010). Statistical learning and language acquisition. *Wiley Interdisciplinary Reviews: Cognitive Science, 1*(6), 906–914.

Root-Bernstein, R., & Root-Bernstein, M. (1999). *Sparks of genius: The 13 thinking tools of the world's most creative people*. Boston: Houghton Mifflin.

Rop, C. J. (2003). Spontaneous inquiry questions in high school chemistry classrooms: Perceptions of a group of motivated learners. *International Journal of Science Education, 25*(1), 13–33.

Rossen, J. (2014, April 10). A brief history of 'Choose Your Own Adventure' [blog post]. Retrieved from *Mental Floss* at http://mentalfloss.com/article/56160/brief-history-choose-your-own-adventure

Rothstein, D., & Santana, L. (2011). *Make just one change: Teach students to ask their own questions*. Cambridge, MA: Harvard Education Press.

Rousseau, J. J. (1762/1979). *Emile: Or on education* (A. Bloom, Trans.). New York: Basic Books.

Rumelhart, D. E. (1991). Understanding understanding. In W. Kessen, A. Ortony, & F. Craig (Eds.), *Memories, thoughts, and emotions: Essays in honor of George Mandler*. Hillsdale, NJ: Erlbaum.

Russ, S. (2003). Play and creativity: Developmental issues. *Scandinavian Journal of Educational Research, 47*(3), 291–303.

Saffran, J. R. (2003). Statistical language learning: Mechanisms and constraints. *Current Directions in Psychological Science, 12*(4), 110–114.

Samuelson, S. (2014). *The deepest human life: An introduction to philosophy for everyone*. Chicago: University of Chicago Press.

Schneps, M. H. (1989). A private universe: Misconceptions that block learning (Video.) Santa Monica, CA: Pyramid Film and Video.

Schwartz, K. (2014a, February 3). Math and inquiry: The importance of letting students stumble [blog post]. Retrieved from *Mind/Shift* at http://ww2.kqed.org/mindshift/2014/02/03/math-and-inquiry-the-importance-of-letting-students-stumble/

Schwartz, K. (2014b, December 15). How 'deprogramming' kids from how to 'do school' could improve learning [blog post]. Retrieved from *Mind/Shift* at http://ww2.kqed.org/mindshift/2014/12/15/how-deprogramming-kids-from-how-to-do-school-could-improve-learning/

Schwebel, D. C., Rosen, C. S., & Singer, J. L. (1999). Preschoolers' pretend play and theory of mind: The role of jointly conducted pretense. *British Journal of Developmental Psychology, 17*(3), 333–348.

Seal, D. O. (1995). Creativity, curiosity, exploded chickens. *College Teaching, 43*(1), 3–6.

Seuss, T., Prelutsky, J., & Smith, L. (1998). *Hooray for differendoofer day!* New York: Knopf.

Shaw, G. B. S., & Winsten, S. (1949). *The quintessence of G.B.S.: The wit and wisdom of George Bernard Shaw.* London: Hutchinson.

Shernoff, D. J., Csikszentmihalyi, M., Schneider, B., & Shernoff, E. S. (2003). Student engagement in high school classrooms from the perspective of flow theory. *School Psychology Quarterly, 18*(2), 158–176.

Shonstrom, E. (2014, June 4). How can teachers foster curiosity in the classroom? *Education Week.* Retrieved from http://www.edweek.org/ew/articles/2014/06/04/33 shonstrom.h33.html

Siegelman, K. (2003). Social studies through poetry. *Journal of Secondary Gifted Education, 14,* 187–188.

Silvia, P. J. (2001). Interest and interests: The psychology of constructive capriciousness. *Review of General Psychology, 5*(3), 270–290.

Simmons, D. (2009, April 1). Main lesson books: How and why [blog post]. Retrieved from *The Home School Journey* at http://christopherushomeschool.typepad.com /blog/2009/04/main-lesson-books-how-and-why.html

Singer, G., & Singer, J. L. (2013). Reflections on pretend play, imagination, and child development: An interview with Dorothy G. and Jerome L. Singer. *American Journal of Play, 6*(1), 1–14.

Singer, J. L., & McCraven, V. G. (1961). Some characteristics of adult daydreaming. *Journal of Psychology: Interdisciplinary and Applied, 51*(1), 151–164.

Smith, D., Wright, C. J., & Cantwell, C. (2008). Beating the bunker: The effect of PETTLEP imagery on golf bunker shot performance. *Research Quarterly for Exercise and Sport, 79*(3), 385–391.

Smith, F. (2003). The immensity of children's learning. In *The Jossey-Bass reader on teaching* (pp. 251–268). San Francisco, CA: Jossey-Bass.

Smith, M. C., & Mathur, R. (2009). Children's imagination and fantasy: Implications for development, education, and classroom activities. *Research in the Schools, 16*(1), 52–63.

Solnit, R. (2007). *Storming the gates of paradise: Landscapes for politics.* Berkeley, CA: University of California Press.

Stein, H. (1991). Adler and Socrates: Similarities and differences. *Individual Psychology, 47*(2), 241–246.

Sternberg, R. J. (1994). Answering questions and questioning answers: Guiding children to intellectual excellence. *Phi Delta Kappan, 76*(2), 136–138.

Sternberg, R. J., & Williams, W. M. (1996). *How to develop student creativity.* Alexandria, VA: ASCD.

Stevenson, K. R. (2007). Educational trends shaping school planning and design: 2007. National Clearinghouse for Educational Facilities, Washington DC. Retrieved from http://www.albanyschools.org/district/Grade.Configuration/Research.docs/Trends.in.school.planning.and.design.pdf

Stewart, J. (2012). The life and work of Kierkegaard as a "Socratic Task" [online lecture]. Retrieved from https://www.coursera.org/learn/kierkegaard

Stinson, L. (2014, April). How to reinvent the school lunch and get kids to eat better. *Wired Magazine*. Retrieved from http://www.wired.com/2014/04/how-to-reinvent-the-school-lunch-and-get-kids-to-eat-better/

Strong-Wilson, T., & Ellis, J. (2007). Children and place: Reggio Emilia's environment as third teacher. *Theory into Practice, 46*(1), 40–47.

Sutton, B. (2009, February 10). Reward success and failure, punish inaction [blog post]. Retrieved from *Work Matters* at http://bobsutton.typepad.com/myweblog/2009/02/reward-success-and-failure-punish-inaction.html

Taleb, N. N. (2012). *Antifragile: Things that gain from disorder*. New York: Random House.

Tarr, P. (2004). Consider the walls. *Young Children, 59*(3), 88–92.

Taylor, M., & Carlson, S. (2000). The influence of religious beliefs on parental attitudes about children's fantasy behavior. In K. Rosengren, C. Johnson, & P. Harris (Eds.) *Imagining the impossible: Magical, scientific, and religious thinking in children* (pp. 247–268). Cambridge, MA: Cambridge University Press.

Taylor, M., Carlson, S. M., Maring, B. L., Gerow, L., & Charley, C. M. (2004). The characteristics and correlates of fantasy in school-age children: Imaginary companions, impersonation, and social understanding. *Developmental Psychology, 40*(6), 1173–1187.

Thompson-Schill, S. L., Ramscar, M., & Chrysikou, E. G. (2009). Cognition without control: When a little frontal lobe goes a long way. *Current Directions in Psychological Science, 18*(5), 259–263.

Tindall-Ford, S., & Sweller, J. (2006). Altering the modality of instructions to facilitate imagination: Interactions between the modality and imagination technique. *Instructional Science, 34*(4), 343–365.

Tobin, K. (1988). Target student involvement in high school science. *International Journal of Science Education, 10*(3), 317–330.

Tolstoy, L. (2015). Who should learn writing of whom; peasant children of us; or we of peasant children? (N. H. Dole, Trans.). Seattle, WA: Createspace Independent Publishing Platform. (Original work published 1862)

Torrance, E. P. (1988). The nature of creativity as manifest in its testing. In R. J. Sternberg (Ed.), *The nature of creativity: Contemporary psychological perspectives* (pp. 43–75). Cambridge, England: Cambridge University Press.

Trabasso, T., & Suh, S. (1993). Understanding text: Achieving explanatory coherence through online inferences and mental operations in working memory. *Discourse Processes, 16*(2), 3–34.

Van Zee, E. H. (2000). Analysis of a student-generated inquiry discussion. *International Journal of Science Education, 22*(2), 115–142.

Vemuri, P., Lesnick, T. G., Przybelski, S. A., Machulda, M., Knopman, D. S., Mielke, M. M., Roberts, R. O., Geda, Y. E., Rocca, W. A., Petersen, R. C., & Jack, C. R. (2014). Association of lifetime intellectual enrichment with cognitive decline in the older population. *Journal of the American Medical Association: Neurology, 71*(8), 1017–1024.

Vygotsky, L. S. (1998). The problem of age (M. J. Hall, Trans.). In R. W. Rieber (Ed.), *The collected works of L. S. Vygotsky: Vol. 5. Child psychology* (pp. 187–205). New York: Plenum Press. (Original work published 1934)

Vygotsky, L. S. (1967/2004). Imagination and creativity in childhood. *Journal of Russian and East European Psychology, 42*(1), 7–97.

Wang, M. C., & Stiles, B. (1976). An investigation of children's concept of self-responsibility for their school learning. *American Educational Research Journal, 13*(3), 159–79.

Watterson, B. (2013, March 17). *Calvin and Hobbes.* Retrieved from: http://www.gocomics.com/calvinandhobbes

Weisberg, D., & Gopnik, A. (2013). Pretense, counterfactuals, and Bayesian causal models: Why what isn't real really matters. *Cognitive Science, 37*(7), 1368–1381.

Werker, J. F., & Tees, R. C. (1984). Cross-language speech perception: Evidence for perceptual reorganization during the first year of life. *Infant Behavior and Development, 7*, 49–63.

Werker, J. F., & Tees, R. C. (2005). Speech perception as a window for understanding plasticity and commitment in language systems of the brain. *Developmental Psychobiology, 46*(3), 233–251.

Wertsch, J. V., & Toma, C. (1995). Discourse and learning in the classroom: A socio-cultural approach. In L. P. Steffe & J. Gale (Eds.), *Constructivism in education* (pp. 159–174). Mahwah, NJ: Lawrence Erlbaum.

White, E. J., Hutka, S. A., Williams, L. J., & Moreno, S. (2013). Learning, neural plasticity, and sensitive periods: Implications for language acquisition, music training, and transfer across the lifespan. *Frontiers in Systems Neuroscience, 7*(90), 1–18.

White, R. W. (1959). Motivation reconsidered: The conception of confidence. *Psychological Review, 66*(5), 297–333.

Wiggins, G. (2013, October 19). Experiential learning [blog post]. Retrieved from *Granted and . . .* at https://grantwiggins.wordpress.com/2013/10/19/experiential-learning/

Willingham, D. T. (2009). *Why don't students like school? A cognitive science answers questions about how the mind works and what it means for the classroom.* San Francisco, CA: Jossey-Bass.

Willis, A. (2006). Ontological designing—laying the ground. *Design Philosophy Papers Collection,* 80–98.

Willis, J. (2012, November 14). *The adolescent brain.* Preconference workshop presented at the Learning & the Brain Annual Conference, Boston, MA.

Wolf, D. P. (1987). The art of questioning. *Academic Connections,* 1–7.

Wood, E., & Attfield, J. (2005). *Play, learning, and the early childhood curriculum* (2nd ed.). London: Paul Chapman.

Woolley, J. D., & Phelps, K. E. (1994). Young children's practical reasoning about imagination. *British Journal of Developmental Psychology, 12*(1), 53–67.

Yackel, E., Cobb, P., & Wood, T. (1991). Small-group interactions as a source of learning opportunities in second-grade mathematics. *Journal for Research in Mathematics Education, 22*(5), 390–408.

Yerrick, R. K. (2000). Lower track science students' argumentation and open inquiry instruction. *Journal of Research in Science Teaching, 37*(8), 807–838.

Zane, L. M. (2015). *Pedagogy and space: Design inspirations for early childhood classrooms*. St. Paul, MN: Redleaf Press.

Zhong, C. B. (2012, November). The role of unconscious thought in the creative process. *Rotman Magazine*.

Zimbardo, P. G., Butler, L. D., & Wolfe, V. A. (2003). Cooperative college examinations: More gain, less pain when students share information and grades. *Journal of Experimental Education, 71*(2), 101–125.

Zion, M., & Slezak, M. (2005). It takes two to tango: In dynamic inquiry, the self-directed student acts in association with the facilitating teacher. *Teaching and Teacher Education, 21*(7), 875–894.

Index

About the Author

 Wendy L. Ostroff, PhD, is a developmental and cognitive psychologist and a professor at the Hutchins School of Liberal Studies at Sonoma State University, a seminar-based program that prepares prospective teachers and emphasizes critical reading, writing, and thinking. The author of the book *Understanding How Young Children Learn: Bringing the Science of Child Development to the Classroom* (2012, ASCD), Dr. Ostroff has been designing and teaching interdisciplinary courses on child development, learning, and education for 15 years, and she offers workshops on applying child development research for scientists and practitioners. She is passionate about innovative and emergent pedagogies and state-of-the-art teacher education.

Related Resources

At the time of publication, the following ASCD resources were available (ASCD stock numbers appear in parentheses). For up-to-date information about ASCD resources, go to www.ascd.org. You can search the complete archives of *Educational Leadership* at www.ascd.org/el.

ASCD EDge®

Exchange ideas and connect with other educators interested in curiosity on the social networking site ASCD EDge® at http://ascdedge.ascd.org/

Print Products

Authentic Learning in the Digital Age: Engaging Students Through Inquiry by Larissa Pahomov (#115009)

Essential Questions: Opening Doors to Student Understanding by Jay McTighe and Grant Wiggins (#109004)

Learning to Choose, Choosing to Learn: The Key to Student Motivation and Achievement by Mike Anderson (#116015)

The Power of the Adolescent Brain: Strategies for Teaching Middle and High School Students by Thomas Armstrong (#116017)

Questioning for Classroom Discussion: Purposeful Speaking, Engaged Listening, Deep Thinking by Jackie Acree Walsh and Beth Dankert Sattes (#115012)

Real Engagement: How do I help my students become motivated, confident, and self-directed learners? (ASCD Arias) by Allison Zmuda and Robyn R. Jackson (#SF115056)

Understanding How Young Children Learn: Bringing the Science of Child Development to the Classroom by Wendy L. Ostroff (#112003)

Online Courses

Sparking Student Creativity: Practical Applications and Strategies (#PD16OC002M)

Understanding Student Motivation, 2nd edition (#PD11OC106M)

For more information: send e-mail to member@ascd.org; call 1-800-933-2723 or 703-578-9600, press 2; send a fax to 703-575-5400; or write to Information Services, ASCD, 1703 N. Beauregard St., Alexandria, VA 22311-1714 USA.

THE WHOLE CHILD

ASCD's Whole Child approach is an effort to transition from a focus on narrowly defined academic achievement to one that promotes the long-term development and success of all children. Through this approach, ASCD supports educators, families, community members, and policymakers as they move from a vision about educating the whole child to sustainable, collaborative actions.

Cultivating Curiosity in K–12 Classrooms:
How to Promote and Sustain Deep Learning
relates to the **engaged, supported,** and **challenged** tenets.

WHOLE CHILD
TENETS

1 HEALTHY
Each student enters school healthy and learns about and practices a healthy lifestyle.

2 SAFE
Each student learns in an environment that is physically and emotionally safe for students and adults.

3 ENGAGED
Each student is actively engaged in learning and is connected to the school and broader community.

4 SUPPORTED
Each student has access to personalized learning and is supported by qualified, caring adults.

5 CHALLENGED
Each student is challenged academically and prepared for success in college or further study and for employment and participation in a global environment.

For more about the Whole Child approach, visit
www.wholechildeducation.org.

LEARN. TEACH. LEAD.